Remote Control Manager

Taking your Career to the Next Level

Jerome L. Hess PhD.

Copyright © 2011 Auth Jerome L. Hess

All rights reserved.

ISBN:
978-0-9836108-0-9

DEDICATION

This book is dedicated to my three most ardent supporters
in business as well as in life

First is Phil Strack,
Phil tolerated my late night calls and stupid ideas,
And ALWAYS said "Awesome idea, Love ya man"
Even though I now KNOW he had to be thinking,
"What a Maroon!"

Next is Joe Pici,
Without whom THIS book would not have made it
to publication

Finally, Charles J. Hess, Jr.,
For not only telling me I could be anything I wanted
For not just encouraging me to be anything I wanted,
For not just showing me that I could be anything I wanted,
But because he loved me and believed in me all along the way.

Table of Contents

Table of Contents..v

Introduction..vii

Foreword..1

Chapter 1: What Kind of Employee do you have?..........5

Chapter 2: GOALS...11

Chapter 3: Keep the TEAM you Have 29

Chapter 4: Searching out your Skills......................43

Chapter 5: Their Resume: What's in it for you?.........47

Chapter 6: Find your Dream Situation.....................51

Chapter 7: What Your Look Says about You............65

Chapter 8: Start Work the very First Day................79

Chapter 9: Staying Happy, Healthy and Wise...........89

Chapter 10: How to get what and Where you want...........101

Chapter 11: Orientation: 111

Chapter 12: 21 Steps for Success........................121

Afterword: 209

Resources: 211

Introduction

This is the second of three books in a series called **The Remote Control Career**, which is culled from over 30 years of documented, hands on provable formulas that have helped advance hundreds of careers.

I do hope that this is not the *third* in a series for you, if so, you may still find a great deal of information here, but you will find that **Remote Control Professional** and **Remote Control Entrepreneur** build upon this content.

I strongly believe that where ever you are in your career quest you will find tools and techniques here that you can carry with you throughout your business and personal lives, as well as think of some other folks in your life, which could benefit from these ideas.

As my mentor once told me, "Don't just write down or think about what I say, instead think about and write down the things that *you* think of when I say what I say."

Now that may seem a tad esoteric, but I promise that is the most ethereal concept you will find here, but it is also one of the most effective tools that I have ever placed in my learning toolbox.

Sit back, and think about where you fit into all this, and equally important, where all of this could fit into what you do!

Foreword

John had fractured his back and couldn't travel as much as his career required. He had spent **ten** years developing contacts, building a customer list and establishing relationships in order to support the customer service that he was raised to expect from a large multi-million dollar company, and in one Doctor's visit it was taken away from him. He would have to start over.

Unfortunately John found it very difficult to find the position that he needed in the 6 figure salary that he was accustomed to, in order to support his family. So he knew he would have to start over.

While his body mended he studied and researched, interviewed and read every business and practice management document that he could lay his hands on. Yet it was the information that he discovered in the most unlikely of places that allowed him to get what he needed.

No, he didn't start at 6 figures, truth be told, he barely cracked 5 ($20,000 a year), but in less than 36 months he was on the fast track back to that $100,000 salary that he knew he needed.

Along the way he found himself in control of more and more people, until he too was in "management." It wasn't a job he applied for, or even one that he wanted, but as your pay increases, so does your responsibility. The one thing that John knew was how to deal with people, and how to put those people together so that they can deal with each other for maximum results

Read **REMOTE CONTROL MANAGER** and find out what John found, that you can manage a team of any size from any location and be successful at HOME and on the job.

Caveat to the Reader: Some folks who read early copies of this book pointed and said "Hey you're talking about me!" After almost 40 years in business you probably will see you somewhere in this book. After all that's why I wrote it. But in all my writing, there have only ever been two real people used in my books. Everyone else is a compilation from one placed in the situation of another. So if you do see yourself, I hope that by the time your done reading, you will be looking at the ideal manager. As for the two real people? Well I'll give you a hint, one of them is me.

Remote Control Management

Jerome L Hess

Chapter 1: What Kind of Employees do YOU have on your team?

Over the last 20 years we have determined that there are 4 different types of employees in the job field, as we go through these brief descriptions, look for the type that most closely fits your style and more importantly look for YOUR team members and this will help you decide in what direction to Move.

To make things easier we will relate these 4 types to the points on our compass, now very few folks fit 100% just one specific type, most of us are a blend, but when you reach the type that you identify with the MOST, that's the type you want to work with.

North – Most employees that are pointing North are either in a leadership role, or they feel they want or deserve to be in a leadership role. Regardless of the pay that goes with it, you're the first one at work every day and the last one to leave, wanting to remain until the last customer has been served. You find yourself reading books and magazines designed to help develop your self esteem, your leadership potential as well as your technical proficiency in your chosen career. When a new project comes up, you're the first one interested because you want to learn everything there is about it, so that you can maintain that competitive edge. You may find that your "leisure" hours are spent attending motivational and leadership events, or listening to the same by cd or cassette or even attending live events. The names Les Brown, Zig Ziglar and Tony Robbins are very familiar, and if you're not reading something they wrote now, you recently have. Your managers know that they can give you a clear set of instructions and let you loose because they know that almost ANY project is safe in your hands! You have NO problem accepting responsibility when things may not go exactly as planned and you will spread the accolades about to your entire team.

South – The Team members on the Southern point of the compass are the "worker bees." These are folks who don't really have any aspiration for Leadership or Management or anything else that your company may term its development programs. You want to come in, perform your 8 – 14 hours of work, and then go home. It's not necessarily that you're lazy; you just have higher interests outside of work that mean more than those inside of work. Maybe you play guitar in a band on the weekends, or fly antique plans, or restore old cars. Your job is what you have chosen to fill those 40 hours a week that will help pay for your hobbies. The good news is that every company in the world needs some folks to fill the southern role. Not everyone can lead, and it's a well established fact that not everyone wants a role in leadership. As long as the Southerners realize that pay increases and merit raises are typically for duty above and beyond the average, they will typically be fairly happy fellows. It took several years for me to understand that not everyone's GREATEST desire is to become a North Pointing Leader! What

I found was that if you had to drag them INTO the role, you will have to continue to DRAG them through every step of the way, and that makes for a frustrated leader and a miserable follower.

East – Now we come to the first part of the blend, the easterners are those folks who are on their way OUT of your team, voluntarily. East pointing folks arrived on your team in one of several ways: 1) They THOUGHT that you did one thing and the reality clashes with their vision SO much that they realize they may NEVER get to do what they want. 2) They saw your team as a stepping stone to something bigger and better. So they are willing to "pay their dues" on your team, while waiting for something (sometimes ANYTHING) to come up that they can move towards. 3) They needed a certain amount of time acquiring a specific skill set so that they could then move on to another team or even another company and do what they REALLY want. I once had a manager who on her first day of work, announced that she needed one years experience doing the job she had at our company, so that she could return to her PREVIOUS employer and get a much bigger promotion. Not something most Easterners want to announce to their leaders.

West – Go West Young Man. That was once the battle cry of a generation of Americans. Today it is a battle cry of a completely different nature. Sometimes you hire a team member who just doesn't fit. Your team, your team dynamics or anything about your company. Sometimes folks know what to say during an interview, and sometimes administration just misses the obvious signs. Either way Westerners are folks who are about to "find themselves voted off the island." Maybe they spend too much time in "social mode" or on the phone or Internet inappropriately, there are a myriad of reasons, and in today's litigious society, most administrators have a great deal of documentation to follow up their decisions, but these west facing folks want to have a very good resume current at all times.

Now obviously this is just a thumbnail sketch of a concept we teach over the course of several hours, and then come back to within its own standalone training, but I think this should give you a pretty good idea of what 'you're' dealing with. Here's the caveat though:

I can't begin to tell you how often someone has gone through our training and not really understood the reason we teach these concepts. This is not some parlor trick that you can whip out at a meeting and say "Well she is always like that, she's one of those darn Southerners." Remember she could say the same thing about those "darn northerners." Don't use these as labels or 'defense mechanisms.' Remember you have complete control over one thing, you. You're not going to change Mary in accounting, but perhaps by understanding a little more about her you can figure out how best to work with her.

I should certainly hope that you can see how identifying your team members, and yourself in these categories would help you help your team work at their utmost and highest.

For example, let's say that you, as the Team Manager have seen in yourself a majority of characteristics that would suggest that you are a Northerner, but your corporate structure requires that you have a Team Lead. Do you really want your Lead to be another Northerner? Well if you want someone who is energetic and ambitious and constantly looking, of course you do! But let me carefully explain, that having a Northerner as your lead can guarantee two things.

1) They are gunning for your job! Imagine they think they want to sit in YOUR chair and get your salary, and your responsibility and you're sleepless nights and...
2) If they are not gunning for your chair they are looking for one just like it. That means that they are not going to be on your team for very long! If you enjoy rotation and training and...well lets just say it could get expensive.

Instead maybe you can't find a lead with some North in them, but they are mostly 'from the South.'

Again, there are Twenty Four solid permutations of how this could mix up and when you include fractional and partials the number goes to infinity (and beyond). So your best shot is to choose the most prominent components of their characteristics and balance them off with your next level of leadership?

What? The next level? Yes you not only need folks who will work well with you, but you need folks who have a team made up of folks that THEY can work with. Now unfortunately in today's work a day world we can't always hand pick every single one of our team mates to make the 'perfect team.' Concessions' will be made but you want to do everything you can to make sure that your team is made up of top quality folks who not only can but want to work together.

Your door can have a sign trimmed in gold that says leader on it, but if no one's following you, who in the world are you leading?

Chapter 2 GOALS

If you are in management or at a point in your career where you seriously want to be in management than goals should not a new idea. If they are then maybe you need to go back and read *Remote Control Professional*. You could be like the young lady whom during our interview we asked, "Where do you see yourself in 5 years?" Her response was "CIO". Now that is a goal, it is also pretty gutsy considering she was applying for the bare bones entry level position that this particular company offered. More about her later.

In **this** section we will break down the process and the meaning behind it, to give you the best perspective we can about why goals are important and how to properly set them.

A very wise man once said that Goals are merely dreams with a date on them. Now as true as that may be, many of us stopped dreaming about the same time we started driving, and never looked back!

If that is indeed true than let's take a minute and get our dream/goal generators 'back on line'!

Forgetting your current situation, be it physical, emotional or financial, if you could do anything in the world, as your job, what would it be? Let your mind wander far and wide? If need be think about those things that comprise your hobbies or off campus spare time, if you can think it, we can find a way to make a career from it.

Step 1. Right now, without delving into too much thought, write down the 5 things you like most to do in your spare time. If this takes more that 2 minutes you're thinking too much. This is a simple exercise and if after 2 minutes you don't have 5 things, than you are getting in the way, so try this: If your boss told you that tomorrow you could have the day off, WITH pay, and you just so happen to have an extra $500 in the bank that you can spend, what would you do? Build a guitar? Work on Models with your 4 year old? Read a best seller? Go Eat at a fine dining restaurant? Write a book you've been thinking about for some time?

There that's 5. Now, let's see what we can do with them:

1. Build a Guitar. Well this one is easy enough to begin, but requires a great deal o patience, fine tuning and attention to details.
2. Build Models with your son?
3. Read a Great book? – By the way. You're NEW habit is NOT to read great books, but instead to read books by great writers! You'll find that makes a HUGE difference.
4. Take your significant other, out to a fine restaurant? – No flip Flops, No Drive Thru's and **no** coupons! That's a start for what makes a fine restaurant.
5. Write a book you've been thinking about for a long time? – WE ALL have at least 1 book running around

in our heads, some more than one! NOW is the time to start!

SO, we're going to write a book. Now what?

Step 2. When will your book be finished?

I know what you're thinking, "**Finished** for crying out loud I don't even have a **title** yet!" You're right, you don't have a title yet, but I know lots of folks who have great titles and no books, so let's try the date first.

Why are we worried about when the book will be done? Because (here's the gem) you must start with the end in mind! Whether you are writing the great American novel or developing a car that runs on tater tots, you must have some solid idea of when you want to debut this to the world!

Why? Because there are hundreds of millions of books that are unfinished because the authors said it would be fun to do 'one day.' I on the other hand am developing a course on writing a book in 3 weeks, so 'someday' isn't in my vocabulary and should no longer be in yours.

When would you like to have this puppy finished? Christmas? Books make great gifts. So okay your now in January, you know that you want to have it ready for Christmas, and given 30 days for publishing, you need it done by the beginning of November and this month has already started, so round it off and let's say 40 weeks. Most good books are in the 200 – 250 page range (hey look how many pages I have) so that means that you need to write 6 ¼ pages each and every week from now until the end of November, that's roughly 1 page every day, each page has about 250 words, even a bad typist like me, that's about 2 hours worth of work.

Now comes the **hard** part, finding 2 hours every day.

Finding the time really isn't that hard, we all have the same 24 hours in each day, so how does Stephen King write (3) 1200 page books a year and we are scared of considering writing one 250 page book this year? Well Mr. King has obviously found a different way to prioritize things that you have. Ok, maybe he isn't the best model to use, after all now he is a full time writer, and has reached the point where a sentence on a napkin will generate enough cash to keep him moving for a year, so let's pick someone else, someone a little closer to home, someone more like you.

Remember we are looking for about an hour a day, and sometimes we won't even need that whole hour. First of all I know you're busy already. You have a job, you have kids, you have a wife, and you have a life to live. Wait you don't have a family? OK try this, you have a car payment you have rent you have utilities, you have...see it's all the same, just called different things.

In another project I developed, I demonstrated that you could in fact write a book by finding just 15 minutes at a time (www.WriteYOURBookin21days.com) . Why 15 minutes? Because we are human, we procrastinate, it will take us 5 minutes to decide were going to write, 5 minutes to get ready to write, and then in 5 minutes I demonstrate that you can with very little thought develop a page of material. I would ask that you check out the aforementioned course as I really don't have the time to go over it all here.

But here's the bottom line. In today's modern world where we have thousands of "things" that our grandparents didn't have, things designed to make our lives easier, we have discovered that these things actually consume the majority of the spare time that our forefathers had to do things like, rest, read and write good material. So in a sense in order to add one thing to our day, we have to find one thing that we can do without! So for one solid day I want you to sub divide your day, hour by hour and write down everything that you do everyday! That is where you will find your time. Whether it's watching TV (that you don't care about) or cruising the Internet, or (heaven forbid) playing PC games, you will discover things that you started to do because you were interested, now you do them purely out of habit! Trust me I know, I found something that I was spending 3 hours every day doing. Typically it's those things that you can do without.

So, you have your time mapped out, during which nothing will ever disturb you, yes I know that's not a reality, but if you involve the wife and kids, you will still be able to find your time. Lunch? After dinner? After the kids go to bed? Now let's move to step 3.

Step 3: The Title of Your book.

If coming up with a title seems a little far fetched, than what's the central theme? The title should be attractive and catchy, but what is it that you want to write about?

There are 2 ways to approach this. First, write about something you know. This is probably the easiest way to write a book, you don't have to do any research; you can just pull stuff from memory. Well OK, it's not that easy, but if you're familiar and passionate about your subject you are already way ahead of the game. Even if it's just something that you're passionate about learning, you still have an advantage. This makes 'creating' the time, much easier than anything else.

The second, and by far, most common method, is to write about something that you have experienced, but perhaps don't know or understand all the details about. The advantage to this is that you will probably have more interest in performing the research and unlike #1 you don't think that you know it all yet. Again, this allows you to use the research phase as your primary motivator for devoting your 2 hours a day.

But you are now well along the path of starting to develop your goals. Please understand that "Goals" is a weekend boot camp in and of itself, so I can not cover it in this chapter completely. However I can tell you that as you lay out your goals you need to do some in 3 "waves".

NOW: Goals you will accomplish within the next 6 – 18 months.

THEN: Goals that you will work on for the next 24 – 60 months

LATER: These are your long term goals, typically these are represented in years, typically 5 to 20 years is an excellent long term goal set.

    As you divide your goals list into these 3 categories you must make sure that each one carries with it a solid, concrete and heartfelt reason of why it must be attained within that time frame. In other words it should hurt if you can not complete these goals on time.

    Next I want you to step way outside your comfort zone, I want you to find the one person who means the most to you, whether it's your dad, your wife, your partner or your mentor, and tell them what your dreams are. Explain to them why these dreams and their proposed dates are important to you and in many cases, how they can be important to them as well.

    You're probably asking yourself "Why in the world would I want to share my dreams with someone else?" Especially when doing so is going to open me up so dramatically to their thoughts and opinions?

    Well there are two reasons for doing this, the first you've already figured out, it's called complete honesty. In order for these goals to have any importance and urgency to you there must be someone else in this world that you feel responsible to, for fulfilling them. See if you set a goal and keep it to yourself you may find it entirely too easy to come up with excuses on why you wont be starting that tonight, tomorrow will present its own set of reasons and before you know it you are on day 89 of your 90 day goal and you never even started. You need an accountability partner, not someone that will nag you to get it done, but someone who understands the importance and the reasons for you fulfilling whatever it is that you have lain out before them! Again, they, must be someone who will feel as disappointed as you do, someone whom you don't want to let down, someone you love and respect.

The other reason, a tad more "logical" (I use that term loosely), is that in all honesty you do need someone to keep you grounded. I can set the goal to play in the NBA all I want, but at 5'-6" 175lbs and 40+ years old, my chances are Awfully Slim. So if one of your dreams is just a little to the left of reality understand that this person that you care about, that you are being completely open and real to, can help you find a way to make something in that arena come true.

Maybe I never will be able to play with Michael Jordan and the Bulls, especially now that he's retired, but if I were in a position where money were not an object maybe I could create a "basketball camp" like the one the kids attend, but this one is just for the "dream teams" of folks who have it their dream as well. Heck I would love to play alongside

Michael in a blacktop street game. Not to mention on an NBA arena! So the goal isn't just playing in the NBA, the real goal is raising enough money so that you could sponsor the basketball camp that would allow you to play alongside him privately!

The dream changes slightly, but the end results are almost exactly what you need!

In reference to where you are and what you do, one of your goals SHOULD pertain to your current job situation. Will you be working with that company 1 year, 5 years, and 10 years from now? My last corporate tenure started as a 1 year rehab for an injury and turned into a 10 year "career change?"

Now remember the young lady who wanted to be a CIO? Well she came across with such a strong sense of self that she was actually able to convince the entire leadership team of this particular company that she was sincere and ready to get started.

Now obviously from zero to CIO In 5 years is a tremendous jump, but it's not unreasonable to be in line for CIO in that time period.

So we sat her down and laid out a 5 year plan. This resulted in 60 month's of weekly goals that she would be able to fulfill, that would then place her in the line she needed to make the jumps she wanted. We even got her a subscription to CIO magazine so she could "read up" on what it took to fill the job.

She is no longer in that entry level team in that bottom rung department, unfortunately she also never fulfilled the requirements that we lay out for her during week one of her plan to CIO. She did generate a series of transfers that were promotions somewhat vertical. But her progress was a snails pace compared to what she wanted. Currently she would have to live to be 167 in order to be CIO. You can lay out everything someone needs, but if they won't take the first step, neither can you!

As a short aside, I do my best to create an open unrestricted **no blame** zone for 30 minutes, every quarter (about 3 – 4 months) throughout the year. I start those meetings the same way every single time with the statement clarifying that nothing said will go beyond those walls. So if the word gets out the only way it did get out was if they told someone..

I follow that up with 2 questions: Where do YOU want to be in 12 months? What would you like to change over the next 12 months?

The reason for those questions is to allow them some time and space for dream building. Now if they start to get too far out on the limb I can start to rein them in, or as happened recently someone clarifies with "what do you mean?" I explain that were talking about career oriented answers and suggestions. This gives me the opportunity to put them on the right track, see how they are following through on our last meeting (keep notes), as well as correct any directions that they may be going in that needs a little course correction.

Realize that these can be dangerous; if you are not the top dog on your totem pole clear it with your top dog. In 30 years of doing this I have only had one time when I was "called on the carpet" for 'pulling people off the floor' for this, until they saw the numbers for the following quarter.

A very wise man once told me, "Jerry if you have to drag them into their dreams, you will have to drag them each and every step of the way." The only thing that does is guarantee that you will always know where you have been. By the series of butt marks in the highway behind you!

Don't be a drag.

So after all of this, are you seeing WHY you will want to have a clear cut idea of your goals? Just in case, try this one on for size. Your team members need to have goals for their future, some will be tied in with yours most will not. But when it comes to helping them develop those dreams that will be the building blocks of their career and this adds to yours. You can't help them if you don't know how to create and manage your own goals.

Advanced Goal Setting

Now, what you have in the previous section is traditional goal setting, traditional in the sense that no matter where you go or who you learn from, you will see many of the same elements in a goal setting workshop. Now we're about to move a little into the twilight zone. I say that because traditionally goals are taught from a very positive angle and the wording and everything about them is traditionally looked at from the "bright side."

What most folks don't teach or even emphasize is that goal setting can be used to help your personal life in a huge way, as well as you public/business life. For example, I make it very well known in my presentations that I am married to one of the greatest women in the world, and that is because of several items, one of which is goal setting. However, when making a goals list for your personal life you need to go a deeper into the advanced techniques. Also understand that if you choose to reveal this information to your SI, you risk being sent to the dog house. I was smart in that I revealed this information while Michele and I were actually in someone else's goal setting workshop. In that atmosphere, it went over very well, others may not be so lucky.

Let me show you what I did. Many people will tell you that there's no real difference between using your business tools in your personal life, and using them in business, I strongly disagree. However I will say that you can use the same standards for your professional life that you do in your business life. But we'll get into that in a minute.

Now, when I say that I had been in one or two relationships that ended badly, I'm not exaggerating. My first marriage lasted 13 months, and started falling apart the week after we got back from our honeymoon. So I knew that in my next relationship I didn't want to duplicate my mistakes. I determined that the first thing was that if my friends don't like her I need to be worried. My friends are a pretty good cross section and if a girl doesn't like one or two, that's one thing, if *no one* likes her, that's a bad thing! So that one may have seemed pretty obvious. However something a friend said to me (afterwards of course, everyone is a Monday morning quarterback), was that she KNEW there would be issues because I am so close to my family and she disliked her own!

Now in retrospect, many people think that "disliked her own" to be a tad harsh, but no, that was actually pretty accurate. So I realized that I had better find someone who gets along with her family really well, as wells as mine. This is what led me down the path of negatives. I had already developed a list of 28 things that my next wife must have, then I started listing all the things that I would not stand for, like not getting along with friends and family. Understandably that was a much shorter list, but it had to be done. When I was done I had 28 positives and 18 negatives, or things that I wouldn't stand for, I've told you about one, but others were not as harsh. For example, I am 100% entrepreneurial based.

Me marrying a school marm, or union rep, would not be a good match.

Although I never thought it was a valid idea, I had heard the concept of 'don't talk politics' it wasn't until college when I found out just how true that could be. I was living with my girlfriend at the time and found out she was on one side of the platform and I was on the other. I didn't think it was a big deal, but she automatically thought that I was an idiot and took every opportunity to state that fact at high volumes. Needless to say, we didn't make it through the primaries.

So how does all this apply to your goal setting? Well what if we started with the opposite side of the coin? Instead of trying to make a list of what the perfect job for you is, how about creating a list of what its **not**! For example, take my last position. I would get up every day at 5:30, wake up my wife up, iron our clothes, shower, shave, take my son to school, drive to w8 to 10 hours I would pick my son up from school, yet I was always very stressed out if anything happened near the end of the day that might make me late to pick him up. Then I'd always spend a portion of my day writing. After I got home I would do some house work, fix dinner, read to the boy, go to bed and start all over again. Monday through Friday. Not to mention all the stupid things I did at work, eat at my desk, stress too much from others, etc. So if I were starting out and looking for a new job or career (as was recently suggested) I could start a list of things I didn't want in that new job, and it might look something like this:

Things I DON'T want in my NEW Job.

1) I don't want to have to get up before 8am
2) I don't want to have to wear a tie
3) I don't want to have to drive 25 miles to work
4) I don't EVER want to worry about being late to pick up my son.
5) I don't ever want to try and work in a 5ft by 5ft cube again
6) I don't want to work for people who have no grasp of how to communicate with others
7) I don't want someone else's poor planning to become an emergency on my part.
8) I don't want to ever work with someone whom I feel like I have to baby sit
9) I don't ever want to lead a team that I don't pick
10) I don't want to have to deal with petty "politics" ever again!

I could continue but I think that's enough. Now I believe that the reason you don't hear about this kind of goal setting often enough is that it would very easily denigrate into a very negative session where nothing good is ever accomplished. But let's use these 10 items as a launching pad to start with.

1) What kind of work doesn't require me to get up early?

   A. shift work

   B. night work

C. telecommuting

D. some types of self employment

2) What kinds of work don't require me to wear a tie?

A. work with a tie less uniform?

B. most types of out door activities

C. telecommuting

D. some types of self employment

3) What kinds of work can I do where I don't have to commute?

A. some shift work

B. telecommuting

C. some types of self employment

D. phone work/consulting/sales

4) What kind of work can I do so I'm NEVER worried about being late to pick up my son from school?

A. teacher at my son's school

B. telecommuting

C. consulting

D. some kinds of self employment

5) What kind of work will NOT restrict me to a small cube?

A. most types of self employment

B. telecommuting

C. entertainment or artistic

D. teacher at my son's school

OK we'll stop at 5, but you can see a pattern developing. Of the 5 answers that I filled in from my 10 questions I am coming up with a few similarities. Almost ALL of the questions were answered with some kinds of telecommuting. There are travel agencies and related industries all over the country that allow you to call in everyday from your house, use your phone and their software and you're good to go.

But then you're still working for someone else.

However, some types of self employment were high on the list as well. So what kind of employment would fit all those other criteria? Well you could become a copy writer? Or maybe an Author, or a research assistant or a medical transcriptionist or an Internet consultant, the choice is yours

So lets see, just from these two refinements what commonalities are we seeing? Well it looks like working from home is playing a pretty big role. You also seem to want to telecommute. Perhaps you have a real affinity for writing, for example, but you aren't sure how to market your writing yet. Get a job as a reservationist or transcriptionist for now, to pay the bills. Meanwhile you can write to your hearts content! All this can be done while you're earning money to pay your bills.

Are you starting to understand how this reverse angle goal setting can work? Are you also seeing why I limited things to nice even manageable numbers? Nobody wants to spend weeks and weeks trying to develop an idea of where you can head, all the while releasing a tremendous amount of the stress you have gathered over the years at your current job. I think you should now have a pretty full tool belt for successful goal setting. Let's see where we should go from here. Also remember that this is something that you should be using with your teams as well. We all have those folks who just are not happy. Well if they will open up to you in your one on one's maybe you can set aside more time for goal setting. You not only get to the root of the issue, but find a solution as well.

Chapter 3: Keep the TEAM You Have

So, you've decided that where you ARE, and the team you're working with is better and pays MUCH better than the unemployment line, smart move. But what SHOULD you do NOW?

Prepare yourself for your NEXT position, either VERTICAL or Lateral and help prepare certain members of your TEAM as well.

1) Make sure your looking at least 1 step up from where you are, preferably 2, OR a departmental move laterally.

I applied for a job once, which I knew I was not qualified for, I wasn't qualified on that day anyway. But I was 100% confident that I could study, during my off hours, hard enough to catch up to become what they needed. At least that's what I thought until I went through the interview. Now let me tell you, the manager that I was interviewing with was thrilled that I wanted to apply, for 2 reasons:

1. This job was 3 levels above where I was, so he was going to get me really cheap, and make his budget look great.
2. He knew, from past dealings that I was the kind of person he wanted in that job. He knew I didn't have the exact skills, but he was very confident that I would get them.

What neither of us counted on was my conscience. I had so much respect for this particular manager that I didn't want to watch his team 'suffer' while I learned the skills I needed. After going back to my desk and spending several more hours calculating the most that they could pay me for this jump VS how much time it would take away from my family, I realized that the trade was not going to be worth it! See on your way up you will have to determine what is and isn't too much of a sacrifice, this is something that only you can really decide: Sometimes the promotion just is not worth it. You should always consult your partner in situations like this; remember there may be more money, but less of you to spend it with! So I wrote him a very nice thank you, for his time, what was scheduled for 30 minutes turned into a 90 minute revelation. Also I found out that other managers in my company valued my skills, far more than I imagined which really primed me for the next opportunity that came along.

Now the best thing that can ever happen in the world during your time in management is to find folks who are as honest as I am. Unfortunately what you will find instead is that your town, as are most, is filled with folks who look at a position like I had. They took one look at the salary, and say I can do that! Without taking serious time to consider what it would truly take, and what they would have to sacrifice, in order to make the job viable. They will accept the job, try hard to make it work and then if it doesn't, someone has a decision to make (that's you).

So it is up to you as a manager to determine where your break even point is, and where you're willing to go to work around it. What do I mean? Well in the example above that particular manager had been advertising nationally (actually internationally) for over a year. They needed to fill the spot with a warm body so that the person who was in that spot before could stop doing 2 jobs at once and costing the company a tremendous amount of money.

That particular manager did something very creative, he promoted from within, gave the job to someone who could learn it in 6 months, but was in no way shape or form, a leader. So, for example, Bob got moved from level 1 to level 2 and the manager hired a Level 3 Supervisor to handle the management portion.

How would you have handled that situation? Here we are 3 years later, the manager in question is no longer in management, and the lead that was hired is no longer in that department and the person who went from L1 to L2 just now got to L3. Over all, the manager made a smart move, however he could have saved his bottom line budget over $100,000 if he had come to that same conclusion during the **first** 12 months, instead of waiting for someone to respond to an ad for a non profit company.

2) PREPARE for the job that you THINK you want, and help your team do the same.

The first time I showed THAT particular piece of the puzzle to someone they were surprised, to say the least, that I would encourage a manager to help his team get ready for a promotion. Of course I would, and so will you, if you're smart.

Most management programs are looking for several things from the folks "getting paid the big money" in their employ. First they want to make sure that you are able to squeeze out every last ounce of productivity from your team. Even the most detached VP understands that the best way to achieve the 1st ideal is to make sure that their employees are happy in what they do and glad to come to work every morning.

Next they are going to look at your team as a whole and watch for two large indicators of a forward thinking manager. The best way they can do that is to ask; "Do you have a plan of ascension?" In other words if they promote you will they now have a huge hole in their staff or are their folks ready, willing and prepared to move up!

Finally your executive staff wants to see some movement occurring in your branch of the organization. If your team, for example, is considered the 'gateway to the corporation' and everyone coming in comes in as a level 1 , that's fine. But if they discover that Frank has been in the same job for 5 years and never been given any more responsibilities, then 1 of 2 things is wrong. Either their manager (you) is not preparing properly for a promotion. Or, their manager (you again) is *not* being very particular when he hires folks and now they are stuck with some great well qualified level 1's who will never be able to move up and out of that chair! That's not a good thing.

So, how do you help your folks find what it is that they want? Assuming they, unlike my interviewee, don't walk in with a 5 year plan to the executive suite. Almost any company worth their weight will have a job shadowing program available, take advantage of it. If your not sure what job shadowing is, every company may treat it slightly different, but in most corporations it consists of you going to your senior manager and expressing an interest in finding out more about what "Sally" does, and you'd like to shadow her for a day. Now if your company doesn't actually HAVE a job shadowing program available they may require that you take off a day of your "paid time off" in order to do this, trust me, it can be a very worthwhile trade off. Realize that this SAME process applies for your folks, however if they are over a certain age, change may not be well received, therefore you may need to step in and do some of the advance work.

1) Now I realize that you will not learn everything there is to know about a particular career in one day of observation, but you CAN prime the pumps, to make sure that it IS the kind of job you think it is.

2) I had a young lady once who had her manager call my manager and ask if she could job shadow me! I couldn't imagine WHY anyone would want that.
    a. At the time, the job I was in was mid level in our company, but entry level for the department I was in.
    b. My "team" was small. OK I was IT, so that's pretty small. Management had been promising me help for MONTHS, and it had never materialized.
    c. We were dramatically overworked. Since I was it, anytime ANY of the teams that I interacted with performed a change (monthly) I ended up putting in 12 hour days for several days straight.
    d. Everyone else in the department had done what we were doing (or so they thought!). See I was brought to this team to strip it down and recreate it from the ground up, into an efficient tight and useful team. Well everyone on the team who was above me got fired, so rebuilding was a must but my organizational skills are what took a great deal of the drudge work out of our processes.
    e. And it had the potential of going from long stretches of boredom to 'the worlds on fire' in the change of a beating heart! Remember what I said about Monthly changes? That was true as long as nothing crashed, but since I work in IT part of our job security is knowing that things *will* crash.

3) Well this young lady came in, right on time, sat down with a notebook, dressed very professionally and asked a lot of questions. <u>always</u> take a notebook with you, the people you're talking to will think you're writing down what they say, thus making them and what they do feel infinitely more important!
    a. Turns out, she wanted out of her department and into mine, and this team was the fastest way for her to do it. She came to the job shadow already knowing that this was going to be what she was going to have to do! In order to get what she wanted!
    b. In the end she turned out to be a huge asset to my team, we streamlined things greatly, and as soon as her 6 months were done (the minimum time before one could transfer) she transferred from my team to a job that she really wanted.
    c. She then spent the next several years doing great things for that company in that department
4) But she had done it the right way.
    a. She knew that she was going to have to spend at least 6 months (or more) on my team. So she came by first in a "scouting" mode to make sure we fit.
    b. As well as making sure that the job itself was something that she was interested in getting involved with. Even though during that one day no major events occurred, I did try and be as honest as I could with her, so as to prepare her for the

worst. There are few things that will kill a team quicker than seeing one partner or the other curling up under a desk in the fetal position, just because things got heavy for a little while.

5) Now you may get some static from your peers for wanting to spread your wings, but that's a good thing. It means you're doing things that they would be uncomfortable doing, it also means you will be the standout. Of course if you put "your foot in it" that's going to stand out as well. Don't you know that your "compatriots" will be the first ones to highlight your errors! If your team thinks that you're going to look bad many of them will be first in line to take a shot at you!

   a. If the 9-5er's who have been watching a clock for 20 years are not in agreement with what you want to do, then your probably doing the right thing!

   b. Additionally if your supervisor should happen to start giving you static that probably means 1 of 2 things:

      1. **ONE:** He sees your value and does not want to lose you from his team. A good leader understands the value of someone who is willing to voluntarily do the unpopular and uncomfortable. Most managers would clone exactly **that** personality trait if they could.

2. **TWO:** You may want to start talking to his boss. If you supervisor is not supportive than he is probably afraid that your activities will be noticed by HIS managers and they will want to know why he only has one person stretching on a team of 20 instead of 19 people stretching with one learning. It may also mean that he's afraid you're going to take his job. At this point, that's a very valid fear!

6). Last but not least, make sure you use that day of shadowing **wisely.** You may not get another shot at it. This is your one shot at learning everything you can by someone who does the job NOW, and not have to WAIT for another opportunity to present itself. If you mess this one up, you could very well make a mess for both yourself and anyone who may come after you that would want to try a team shadow.

   a. In addition to asking lots of questions about the duties performed, make sure you ask about the rest of the things that go with it! Is "on call" expected from every team member? Typically how long would a new person have before certain milestones (like on call) would be expected of them. Is there the opportunity for additional learning and educational experiences? Many companies love continuing education; they just don't have any money to pay for continuing education.

b. Make sure that you ask plenty of questions about the entire team. Including the Team Lead or whomever you will be receiving the majority of your daily marching orders? How many will there be on the team? Will you have the opportunity to train with everyone on the team or will the majority of your training be with just one person? The more differing views you can get, the better prepared you will be when you're by yourself!

c. Realize you will be spending over 2000 hours a year with these folks, in many cases, that's more time than with your spouse, so please take time, and ask some questions, the answers of which are important to you, and make sure that it all fits. One of my former managers and I determined that we could teach anyone the technical aspects of what they needed to do to be successful on our team. What we were interviewing for was a balance and a fit with the rest of the team. Also this manager was very smart, she interviewed with herself and two other team members so she could always have a mix of opinions. This would help her choose, and often times help her "vote" on how a particular candidate did.

3) Perfect the COMMON skills uncommonly!

For several years I was involved in the hiring process of a corporation, for whom we did technical work, but the technical part could literally be taught to anyone, however the customer service aspect was something that could not be taught, you either had it or you didn't. Additionally the ability to manage customer *expectations* was <u>vital.</u> If you could not handle someone screaming at You, and not only talk them back from the ledge, but make them think your a genius for doing so, I didn't have a job for you. But managing expectations was much more than just managing a customer. You must know that you can not use words like "I can" or "I will" or "we must", because in the customers mind you have just made a time and resource commitment for resources that you may not have any control over.

Truthfully those are still skills I look for in people I do business with. Unfortunately they are not skills that are being taught in college. Having spent many years in those hallowed halls of upper education collecting several "pieces" of paper my self, I can tell you that college is trying to prepare you to get a job, but college can not prepare you to maintain or to succeed in a job once you have one!

So find out what skills are most important in your dream job and work on those, not the ones that you're told are the most important. For example, you come into an area where the manager is interrupted four or five times a day by their boss, who looked to be "just checking in." Due to this constant barrage of unexpected interruptions your boss is always on edge waiting for the "other shoe to drop." As the new guy your desk is right next to the door to the office "So security doesn't have to walk you too far." When you see your manager's boss come through the door, shoot her instant message saying "Bob's on his way," you will be thanked! Now you know the skill you need, you must pay attention to what's going on and make sure that your boss doesn't get any 'surprises.' You will find that this slowly turns into a reliability relationship where your manager starts to 'count on you.'

Some managers take a little more training than others. I had a VP running through a building one day looking for "*Any Manager in the building*" because the power went out. So I emailed MY new manager (who was at lunch) and said hey, "just so you know XYZ is looking for any manager because of ABC." He emailed me back and said "What am I supposed to do about it, I'm at lunch?" (Not a *professional* reply in any circumstance) I calmly replied and said "I just didn't want you to get surprised by it when you walked in the building.

He apologized when he returned and thanked me for the heads up. Apparently he had been eating with my former manager who explained that I was trying to keep his butt from catching fire when he first walked in.

So far what we have been working on is your job prospects. The one thing that you have to remember is that if you have sharp folks on your team, and you wouldn't have gotten to management if you weren't sharp. They are thinking the same thing that you are. This is not necessarily a bad thing, if your upper management sees that you are perpetually creating leaders they will start developing a great perspective of you and your methods.

Alternatively, they may also be seeing that a huge chunk of your budget, whether it's on a spreadsheet or not, is being invested on training, because every time one of your folks gets a promotion you need to train someone else to take that persons job! So lets make sure that IF your team is transferring out they are going somewhere where they will be successful at what they do.

So let's look at your team:

Chapter 4: Searching out their Skills

When looking for a new job, either in the company you're in or elsewhere, always remember one VERY important fact of life: **Sometimes the *getting* is better than the *having*!**

This applies to you wanting to be in management as well as to you bringing in team member to fill out the team that you have. When you are recruiting, what exactly are you saying? Now, most folks have become hyper-sensitive to what they say in an interview, because their never sure who may be listening, but what about when its just "the two of you?" I had a boss once who had ben married to the same woman since High School, when, at age 35, she decided to leave him, he went through mid life crisis in a huge way. I was the one he told ALL the companies secrets to, I was his confident for the girls he dated (T.M.I.). For whatever reason he created a bond between the two of us that I really expected to carry through to work the next day.

Then he came in hung over the next day. Guess what else I was? I was the youngest guy there, I was low man on the totem pole, I was…..expendable, or so he thought. About once a week he would fire me, and then wake up the next morning and not remember anything and call me up wondering why I was late to work. It can be a very tough thing to do, separate friends and his work relationships. You don't always have to keep them separate. As long as you both know where the line is drawn, and you know when to talk and when not to, you shouldn't be a strong silent type. You should be you, just monitor what it is that makes you positive and where your values lie, in respect to where your job is

Also, are you sure that's the job you've always wanted? What is it about that particular job that just screams to you *this is the perfect place for you!!!!!* Have you ever worked in that industry? Do you know anyone who works in that industry? Can you take a day off from your current job and go shadow someone in that industry without your current boss knowing that you're looking? Unless you have an *amazingly* good relationship with your boss, typically relating the information to him, that you would like a day off so you can go shadow another career in another company will result in you having lots of spare time to shadow whatever career you want as your primary employer will most likely free up about 40 to 50 hours a week for you.

What we're getting at; is how can you find out if what you think you want to do will have any relation to what you will ever actually be doing? Corporations all over this country are filled with folks who applied for job **X** and ended up performing tasks that were completely unrelated with what they thought the job was that they were hired to perform.

In my last position alone, at least half of my fellow analysts were in the same situation. This actually resulted in a pattern of exodus from that particular company. To make matters worse, the administrators had no recognition of the fact that this was occurring, and were therefore spending 10's of thousands of dollars in training every quarter to ready team members who wouldn't last out a year.

So, in whatever form or fashion you can find for your prospective and present teams, find a method that actually demonstrates for them what they are doing on a day to day basis. Telling an analyst that they will be merging patient data in a Series 11 Mainframe sounds pretty impressive, compounding that description with the fact that it must be done in less than 15 minutes, adds a sense of excitement.

But when they find that 8 hours a day 5 days a week they are highly paid data entry clerks with no allowance or tolerance for data analysis, they will become very unhappy, very quickly. If this happens one of several things will follow, either they will become bored and their work will suffer. Or, worse yet, they will become bored and others work will suffer.

Find a way to really expose yourself and your teams to what they and you will be doing every day, day in and day out. If you are afraid that they won't like it, guess what, **you're right**. But at least if they don't start, you wont have an educational hole in your budget that you could drive a truck through, instead you may just have to look a little harder.

Now, if you're uncertain how to do that, read on and I will outline for you exactly what you want to do to make sure that the employees you interview are the ones you want to work with and that those are the ones you hire to work with you and your team!

Chapter 5: THEIR resume: What's in it for you?

What is important in your resume, and what to look for in theirs.

1) Don't **LIE** – you will be found out, sooner rather than later, and now you not only won't have a job, but now you don't have much of a reputation either. As a manager you are at a small disadvantage now days when verifying information. EEOC states that you can only ask **X** questions about Y subjects and anything outside those boundaries don't have to be answered and can get you in trouble for asking. So what can you do? Well without talking to a lawyer, how about:

   a. Find something in the resume that you either have intimate knowledge of or that you can find intimate knowledge of and ask them a question, relating to your job, about their previous position that they would have only known if they were actually working it.

   b. Look on the web, find some of the "officers" and mention them in passing. "Oh I see you were at APC INC. You know their CEO John just loved to play golf, did you ever get to play on that course….

   c. Or a job specific; "Wow it says here that you have experience on the system 3700 that's great, I was going to install one of these here, but when I found out….."

2) Don't let your exaggerations get out of hand. – It's a commonly held belief that everyone stretches the truth slightly in parts of their resume. It's when the truth breaks and you keep right on going, that you have opened yourself up for a world of bad things.

- **a.** When building your teams, ask yourself just how much leeway you're going to allow? As I suggested we all have some exaggerations, but I have seen resumes that look like they were 5th grade answers to Creative Writing assignments.
- **b.** Ask someone else (your team Lead or Supervisor), one step above or below you, to look over the resumes. Sometimes others will see something that you might miss 100 times over.

3) If you have some skills that you haven't taken the time to label, now is the time to do so. – If you were the bouncer at a nightclub, but your clients were strictly high profile celebrities, than you probably did less talking with your fists and more negotiating and redirecting with your people skills.

- **a.** You need to use examples where you can – If you have a new skill set that you just created a label for, the best thing you can do is use specific examples of HOW these skills were applied then. More importantly how they would be applied in the new job and be an asset to your prospective team.
- **b.** Maybe you never held the title of manager or supervisor, but if you were the senior member of small groups don't be afraid to find a way to use

that in your resume. Maybe you were a Lead or SME (subject matter expert) for your group

c. Were you the one person your boss trusted to schedule her meetings and appointments and interviews? Than maybe executive scheduler isn't too far outside the realm of possibility.

Alternatively you also need to create a series of key words and skills that you know should be used in the resume of someone applying for your position who has worked in your field before. For example, if your looking for a Lead Field Network Technician, he's probably going to pepper his resume with technical terms and specifications, but when it comes to leading and developing a team, his vocabulary should reflect the size of team that he is working with.

The one thing that you **do not** want to do is use terms that imply any education or professional certifications that you can't produce. We all know that there are industry "buzzwords" that can be used to catch people's attention. We also understand that some of those phrases imply a professional standing that needs to be demonstrable.

For example if you were the person that your boss sent to all the classes to learn the new software package you may consider yourself the **Subject Matter Expert**. However, unless you have a class completion certificate, naming those classes individually could imply a higher education as well as become a very boring read.

Another case in point, I spent a year working as a fry cook in a restaurant. Now this was a pretty high volume restaurant and occasionally we all had to do each others jobs. But for me to put down Head Cashier and Host is just plain wrong. To say that I developed some high pressure "cash handling experience" would be stating the right thing at the right time! Now to be honest, that restaurant doesn't even exist anymore, so how could my new employer ever find out? Well that all happened in a very small town and folks knew what Jimbo's was, even if they'd never set foot inside!

You can take some liberty to develop your experience into something that better fits the job you're applying for, but remember there may well come a day when you are expected to demonstrate your skills under a completely different type of stress than what you are accustomed to. Make sure you're up for the job!

Again, you want to watch those skills that your team members are using on their resumes that just do not seem to match up with what they say they did. For example if they say that they were the Lead Sales professional in their High End A/V room and he lists the name of a store you know only pays commission and yet his income peaked out at $10/hr you can start thinking that there may be an incongruity there. Only you can determine what kind of tolerance you can accept on such ideas, but remember if the will falsify some small information to get in the door, would they then falsify some other numbers on a data trending report?

Chapter 6: Find THE dream situation
For you AND your TEAM!

Whether it's where you ARE or where you need to GO

There is a VERY old leadership technique that dates back farther than probably this country, it's now known as the "Ben Franklin Technique" and it involves making a list of the good and bad aspects of a decision and comparing them, invariably one will definitely overshadow the other. I propose that you take THAT one more step forward!

Step 1 - Awareness – Be AWARE of WHAT you believe:

We all have certain beliefs about things (money, careers, relationships), and those beliefs are rooted very deeply inside of us, but they were never designed to become oldie von Moldie ideas that develop into these 'written in stone' foundational blocks of what you believe! Instead your business beliefs should be flexible, fluid, and very transitional. But be careful, because I believe that if we all examine our belief centers, we may find certain things that we think we believe in, that just simply are no longer true. Be flexible and be willing to change your beliefs. Equally important of course is your ability to actually see what's in your **own** belief window. Some folks actually have a set of "beliefs" that they have built up inadvertently over the years, and they are imposing these beliefs on other people without actually have taken anytime to examine and cut down on the beliefs and whether they are still relevant or not!

Now that you have your belief window cleared we need to start working on exactly what it is that you want. This process can be used to select a new job, move ahead in a job you have, or even in family relations. Just as important however, this same process, when correctly applied, can help your set goals for the folks on your team, or at the very least, point them in the right direction.

Let's start with your career. Get a pen and a piece of paper and just open your mind, begin to write down every single thing that YOU can come up with that would be a hallmark of the perfect job for you! For example:

Step 2 - Will you be working for yourself or someone else?

    a.   If for yourself what industry?
    b.   Will you be starting a business or buying a franchise?
    c.   If a franchise where will the money come from?
    d.   If a business, what industry will you focus on?
    e.   If you're working for someone else will you be working in a strength you currently have?
    f.   Or will you be willing to start over and take the pay cut that a decision like that will bring with it?
    g.   If you're taking a pay cut are there others involved that you should consult with? (Wife. /partner, parent, etc.)

Step – 3 - After you decide who to work for:

Once you have decided (for example) to work for someone else you're still not through. Let's assume however that in making this decision you chose an industry as well.

1. Is this locked into one geographical area or are their openings everywhere?
2. If you can go anywhere, would moving be a cost effective way of starting in that career?
3. How much movement is there in that industry?

Step – 4 – You Know what and Where –

Now you have decided you want to work in an industry and where you want to live:

1. Do you want to go with a huge multi national conglomerate or a small mom and pop?
2. If you're going with a large company, have you ever worked in a "cube" environment?
3. Is that something that you find conducive to your lifestyle and beliefs?
4. If you're looking at a smaller style of employment are you comfortable with the restrictions that there may be on your movements?
5. If the company is family run are you OK with almost always being looked at as the outsider?

Step – 5 – Who Will your team be?

Now it's time to think about WHO you will be working with:

1. Describe your perfect boss.
2. Do you have a gender issue? Or perhaps you just work better with one than another?
3. Ask about the companies "yearly" convention, awards banquet etc. If you're in step 2 of 12 and their yearly awards banquet is a drunken brawl, perhaps this isn't a perfect match for you!
4. Do they allow, or does it matter, smoking? Many employers have "help" available to quit smoking, but some just expect when you walk in the door, its not to be noticeable – by whose judgment?
5. Don't be afraid to interview your boss, please try to remember he is interviewing you! Make sure that the fit is there!

Step – 6 - Now do the exact opposite.

1. For every item you have listed, I want you to find your exact opposite. For example, list the qualities of the worst manager you have ever had, and what made them that way.
2. Which of these are you absolutely **not** willing to compromise on?
3. Remember if you are willing to compromise your beliefs for a job, then they are not very strong beliefs now are they?

4. Most people will find in very short order, that once they begin to compromise any of their belief structure for a paycheck, that paycheck will very soon, no longer be enough!
5. Be flexible, but do not break your own rules!

Now that you have 2 very long lists of things that you will and will not have in your working environment, number them, from 1 to whatever, and order them in order of things that you can be somewhat flexible on, down to things that you would never be willing to budge on.

Narrow down the list and now you should have a very accurate description of your perfect working scenario. Your job is now to find the position, company and staff that match **closest** to what you want!

Remember if you have a list of 29 things you must have, and they aren't items you're your willing to bend on, if you find a job that fits 28 of them, don't wait it out. You could see the greatest jobs flash right before your eyes and not know it.

After you have made your list, ordered it and checked it twice, your last instruction is to look back, and in your working life, is there any situation, where, knowing what you know now, you would not get involved, regardless of the outcome? Now you have a clear idea of exactly what it is you want, and even some ideas on how to find it.

Your last step: Find it!

So, now you have done MORE than your due diligence, and you know that this (whatever this may be) is exactly the industry you want to be in, now what? Have you looked at the jobs, yes all the positions that you are likely to need to occupy between the days you start work and the day you finally get to that coveted dream job, have you examined all of those from every angle? For example if you're an engineer who has always wanted to be a Chef, chances are you're going to be in the prep cook position for quite a while learning the basics. Is that something you are prepared for? Are you ready physically, mentally, emotionally and most of all **financially**? Yes financially, how long can you afford to BE a "prep cook", and will your current lifestyle adjust to that? If not, what adjustments are you willing to make in order to make it happen?

First thing you need to do is an honest evaluation of yourself. Not just your good points either, but all your points. For example, I may have the technical expertise as well as the customer relationship skills that every IT manager dreams about for his Field Technicians, but at my age and physical conditioning, if I am expected to move 80lb CRT's and 50lb laser printers all day, while covering a campus wide area that covers 3 city blocks even I have to say no from the start. Could I do it? Possibly, but I know I would work up such a sweat doing it that I'm going to look like a homeless man and smell like the dog in a rainstorm at least by lunch time. So now that's not fair to me or the boss.

Additionally what are your skill sets for that job? I don't mean what schools have you been to, there are several jobs that pay a decent wage that rely on MANY skills other than those taught by your local university.

1. Customer service for example. As we talked about earlier, that is vital in so many jobs, but if you freeze up like an 8 year old in the 3rd grade school play every time a customer starts taking out their lack of planning on you and your department, well maybe that's not a perfect fit either!
2. Do you have some skills that you're not using? Maybe you had a side class in school that you absolutely loved, but your dad said there was no money in it, so you set it aside and pursued the primary goal. What were those other skills? How could they be turned into a side career? A very good friend of mine, never found the time, or money, to make it through college, but her ability to just "pull together" an outfit, gave her a tremendous edge when she went to start a "Vintage Clothing business." Heck I'm a guy, color blind and fashion stupid, but when I need help I certainly know who I can turn to! So what can you do, that is fun, but you never thought you could make money at? We'll find a way to turn that into a career or at the very least a set of skills that will get you in the door!
3. What skills are you using in the job that you have? This may seem obvious, but were going to come back to it several times (maybe meaning that it has

special significance?). Just because the plaque on your door, or name badge or what have you, says you're the left handed noodle squeezer for the Spaghetti corporation, what else do you do in your job, that could be a marketable skill? We all do things through out our work day that we may not ever consider, yet our management hierarchy couldn't do without! For example, I attended a class 10 years ago, in a subject I had **no** interest in, but it was a class being paid for by the company so why not, a week out of the office , you didn't get those very often! It turns out that 2 years later after there had been HUGE turn over in our corporation, I was handed an assignment that I had to complete before I could accept a promotion. Talk about God loving the simple minded. The core of that entire project revolved around that class I had taken 2 years earlier, and wasn't sure how I would ever use those skills. If I told you how often, something like that saved me at the nick of time you would swear I was making them up. Proves you have to pay attention in class!

4. Which skills are you not using that you could be using? Look we all have something in reserve, that little extra boost, or that small additional skill set that you learned along the way in some other company. What are you saving it for? Find a way to make it work for YOU now! Look at it this way, restaurants know for certain that customers like to

get things for free. They also know that their highest margin (the things that cost them the least) is desserts. What one item will most Americans who are paying for a meal in a restaurant skip? Dessert! So by "giving" you a coupon for a free dessert with every adult meal purchased, they have just guaranteed that everyone who leaves will be a lot fuller than they might have been AND they will feel that they got a tremendous bargain. So what skills do you have that you have been holding back? You already work for your employer, so they are already paying for the meal, now what's the bonus? What is going to make your manager bring your name up the next time he has lunch with his manager? Those are the skills that you need to dig for and start using on a daily purpose every chance you can!

OK, so you have gone through an honest Re-evaluation of yourself, hopefully it's not your first, because it certainly won't be your last.

Next you need to do the one thing I find extremely difficult, now you need to re-write your resume. There are almost as many different "styles" of resumes as there are people who have written them. Everyone thinks that their way is the best way, although there are some things that you want to watch for, and things to avoid, anyone who thinks that they have the absolute best resume style to use is saying so because the last time they wrote their resume that's what they used. One thing to prepare yourself for is, if you're shy prepare yourself for someone you know to read and comment on your resume. Spell check is great, but if you spell a word correctly, that is actually a word, but it's not the form you wanted, don't be surprised when someone asks where *Forte Lauderdale* is in Florida.

Also, by having others read and comment on your writing, you are better prepared for what may happen once that same resume gets in the hands of the folks that will be questioning you about its contents. A good editor will do several things, obviously they will look for the glaring errors, and they can also let you know if something is just a touch too long or perhaps even too brief. They can also let you know if the way you have expressed yourself in your resume truly represents you as you wish to be represented. Remember several folks from the company that you want to work with may have the opportunity to see your resume before it ever gets in the hands of the person conducting the interview.

Spelling and grammar errors will be the death of even a great resume. I had a great boss once, this lady was a joy to work with and work for, but if she was reading your resume, she would stop reading after your 3rd spelling or grammar error. She was a former grade school teacher who actually left the school system because she couldn't deal with how poorly teachers were being allowed to perform their jobs. She certainly was not going to tolerate the obvious product of that failure in her workplace.

Also, when you have another set of eyes focused on your resume they may be able to give you some ideas that you haven't thought about yet. Remember no man, or woman is an island, with as many folks out of work as there are now, people have lots of great and some not so great ideas on how to market you. Many of these just won't fit you or what you want to do. For example a resume on pink linen with a sachet probably won't fly if the job you're applying for is that of diesel mechanic. However, if you're local Assembly of God church needs a new IT guy, and the person in charge of HR is the wife of the Sr. Minister, that could be the perfect opportunity to show your creativity!

One of the most difficult parts of re-writing a resume when you are looking for a job is that you need to have several different styles of resumes. Each one tailored for the specific industry in which you will be applying. For different reasons, they may not even look like they came from the same person. For example, if you are looking for a job in an office in the data entry field, you will be drawing on every job that you have had, that could even remotely apply. Then you will be highlighting all of the skills that you learned that would be of any interest in the data entry field.

On the other hand if you are also applying to your local restaurant as a prep cook your ability to type 80 words per minute is not a skill that they care about. So you will instead highlight everything that you can that would relate to that industry.

But what if you're changing careers entirely? Then what do you do? Well funny thing you should ask. My brother, who is 10 years older than I am, recently determined that his health could no longer support him in restaurant management, and a change was required. Starting his "day" at 7pm and ending it at 5am 7 days a week, was NOT something that his body could maintain into old age. So he needed not just a new job, but a whole new career. Well it turns out that one of the restaurants that he had worked in had used his decades of experience to "flip" their restaurants. He was the hired gun, brought in to turn around a restaurant that had a great product a great location and almost NO foot traffic. So when he wanted to get into a management career he highlighted all the successes that he had with turning his restaurants around, working with people, hiring and firing and dealing with many of the other tasks that went alongside the 'turning around' of a restaurant. He highlighted those skills and soon he had three major corporations, waiting for him to produce for their companies.

Therefore he had to slightly alter the focus of his resume to look at his people skills and management style more and look away from his restaurant business and bar skills less.

Now most of the focus here has been on YOU and your search, but the best part about ALL of this information is that it is the same information that you can use to help your team members find out exactly what it is that THEY want. Additionally you can use these same types of exercises to help find out who really should be lasting through the 90 day probation period and who will not!

In one of the larger companies that I worked, they would *insist* that every single person whether they were an IT manager or a Grounds Keeper Manager take X number of managerial classes within the first 90 days of their being hired. Typically that meant that any new manager wouldn't see much of their teams until their third month in the job.

What many of us who knew we wanted to be in management started doing were finding out how many of these classes they could, before they even started applying.

Why am I telling you all this? Because you need to understand that your companies will give you a certain amount of leeway in how you treat your new hires, as long as you can express to them that you are doing something very productive, that should be saving the company money in the long run. Corporations may not know how to save a million dollars this year, but if you can show them how they can do it over a span of ten years and they will be all ears!

So develop better teams, develop a plan of ascension and demonstrate to your management how this will save them hundreds of thousands of dollars, or at the very least,. Make them look better than the guys down the street and you will be named the head of your own brand new program!

Chapter 7: What your "look" says about you, and your team.

Or, what you look like when you look like you're looking!

Regardless of whether you want to move up or move out, here are some tips that you'll need to know!

Dress for the job you <u>want</u> not the one you have or are applying for. There has been an entire industry of books tapes and seminars on how to "Dress for Success", and maybe you have read them and maybe you haven't. But I would like to change that a little. In my office we dress for the job that is at least 1 if not 2 levels above the one that we want! If I'm applying for a counter position at Burger King, guess what, if all of their management staff wears ties and shirts with collars that are ironed, than when you go for your interview, <u>so should you</u>. Once you get the job, let your boss tell you that you only need to wear XYZ. Just make sure he knows you're prepared to wear you're tie! Remember, if you dress up properly, you can always scale down once your there. Guys can take off a jacket, so can gals. Women have many other options available. But the ideas are all then same!

Let's say that you're applying for a job in a national call center and the company dress code is "business casual", you note that most everyone on the floor interprets that as an open necked golf shirt and slacks. What should YOU do? Well if your goal is to stay on the floor answering phones for the next 20 years, you need to stock up on khaki's and golf shirts. But since

I know you want more, you need to look around and see what is being worn by the folks at least 2 pay grades above your spot. In this case that would not be the team lead, but the floor manager. You know him, the guy in charge of 400 employees. Notice, is he wearing a Tie? He probably is. Are his slacks casual khaki's or professionally pressed dress pants? Is he wearing "dark sneakers" or hard shoes that actually take a shine? Whatever it is, model that behavior, until you own that position!

A side note on shoes. Unless you are a kindergarten teacher, make sure your shoes have laces that are the right length, the right color and that they are tied. I can not tell you how often I see some guy (20 something's, usually) spend several hundred dollars on a pair of XYZ Sneakers, only to see him walk around the office with his shoes untied! Now first of all, if your 20 something and your spending THAT much on sneakers, you have a serious priority issue. Next if you're not even going to take care of them properly, that is just beyond my understanding. But more importantly, it looks incredibly *sloppy*. You can not make that look good. I don't care what rapper/basketball player/etc. is wearing them, you are not him, the chances of you being him, or being in his "shoes" someday are about 16 billion to 1. I'm quite sure that your boss is also NOT looking to hire that guy, or he would be calling around on his family tree. So tie your shoes!

Now, back to the important stuff!

On occasion however you will sometimes find that putting yourself in the position of dressing better than the rest can be precarious. For example, I was part of a company once and deliberately came in at the bottom level, even though I was at least 10 years older than my front line managers. But there was NO way I was going to try and go the way of their "trendy" chino look that all the managers seemed to sport. I was however, able to take their look and "age it" a little to be more appropriate for someone of my stature (I don't have a 19" waist anymore). By applying that maturity level, I stood out, with zero additional cost, and gave a perceived added value to what I was already doing! Not surprisingly, to me anyway, within my first 90 days I received my first raise, and then 60 days later my second raise and first promotion. What was it that differentiated me between the rests of the applicants? According to my manager, I projected a professional excited attitude of someone who came to win! This came through my dress and attitude 100% because there were many other folks applying who were far more skilled than I was at the technical aspect of that job.

Whenever dress is brought up, everyone worries about money, the image of going to the mall and spending hundreds of dollars on a new wardrobe inevitably flashes through most men's eyes. Most women are thrilled with the idea, even though their budgets may not approve of their investing in a new wardrobe. So try these options: Even Target sells dressier clothes. Now I am not recommending you buy your suits at a store that only has Small Medium and Large, but they have a good selection of Ties, and Belts that can save you a lot of Money.

Which brings me to an important point; the two biggest eye sores that most men neglect are our **belts and shoes**. These are areas that will stand out like MUD on a white pony, <u>Do Not</u> make that mistake! If the finish starts coming off your belt replace it! People know that times are tough, but they also know that belts ought to be tougher, and if they aren't, then maybe you're buying the wrong kind. Remember no animal was ever harmed in the harvesting of pleather, but many a job interview was. As for shoes, even if you have a pair of *interview* shoes, that you only wear for interviews, that's fine, just make sure they are well kept, shined and clean! However do not be like the guy that tried to slide one past me, wore great shoes, but no socks. Even though I voted no on this prospect, my boss wasn't swayed by his lack of socks. Not so surprisingly security escorted him from the building 6 weeks later.

Back to clothing options, I remember once I went to put my suit on, and did not realize that something in the closet had gotten knocked over by a cat, and 30 minutes before I had to have it, my coat had a huge stain on it. The way I saw things, my options were rather limited, I could: panic and not wear a jacket (not a good idea). Or I could take the $10 I was going to use for lunch and swing through the Salvation Army on my way. There are some very nice thrift stores in this and any other town, and in the case of the Salvation Army, for example, you are actually helping out a very good organization. Most thrift stores clean all their clothing professionally before it's put out for sale. Make sure yours is. You do not want to project the image of a smoker if you are not one. No let me re-state that. You do not want to project the image of a smoker even if you are one. My company recently became a 100% smoke free campus for guests AND employees. It has gotten so stringent that other employees are encouraged to turn you in if you go out to lunch and have a cigarette in the car on the way back to work! Regardless of your personal opinions there are many reasons why this is a good policy. We are a self insured corporation. We can't ask the guests to walk 6 blocks down the street to light one up, if our own employees are sitting in the garage with a lit cigarette. Think of all the lost time your boss would have to put up with if he had to let you run down the street (6 blocks away) every time you wanted to light up!

Now let's address my least favorite part of these conversations, women's dress. Look I admit I am color blind and Fashion Stupid, most men are. But after interviewing hundreds of female professionals here in the Southeast here are several hard and fast "suggestions" for the ladies. If I were you I would take that word "suggestion" exactly as it is intended. **First,** If you would wear it on a night "out" don't wear it to work. You're not trying to seduce someone at work (or you shouldn't be anyway) so let's not look the part. Many men won't respect you, and many women (who are now in the majority in many corporations in management) won't take you seriously.

I was in a technical position once with 2 women working on the same team; both were in their mid twenties, both very attractive. Both of them were very intelligent, respectful and modest ...well almost. One of these young ladies, dressed fairly conservatively, and therefore garnered a great deal of respect both from her co workers and those of many other teams. The other young lady was from a fairly exotic heritage, and liked to dress to emphasize that. She wore lots of long sleeved very flowing blouses and had miles and miles of beautiful thick hair, that she always wore down.

Needless to say, she was a favorite among her male team mates, but when it came promotion time, she never received the promotions that she thought were due her. Her raises were never quite as high as she would have liked; and her career actually seemed to stall for several years.

In a closed door conference with her manager, while discussing promotions I actually questioned her manager on why things seemed to stall for this particular individual. Remember when I said this was a technical position? This job required that she put her hands in very tight; dirty places with lots of sharp corners, her male counterparts, feeling she might hurt herself, always seemed to volunteer to help her in those jobs.

It turns out that her manager had actually counseled her on the dangers that her clothing presented in the workplace and how it and her hair, might better be configured for this particular position (and the next one that she was eligible for), yet nothing ever changed.

HINT: If your boss tells you to change, don't just take it as a subtle suggestion, *Make it happen*.

Skirts, they can be very professional and speak volumes about the person wearing them. But they should be at or below the knee, no questions asked. Any shorter and your back in night club territory and that's not where you want to be. If all you have are micros and minis, dress slacks are a perfectly acceptable alternative for most women.

Finally: If you are wearing a dress or skirt, you need to be wearing pantyhose. Hey, I know I live in the Southeast, I know its 98 degrees with a heat index it feels like 106, but it's your choice, if you want to be treated like a professional, dress like one. That means hosiery.

Remember the "at or below" the knee? Well I did run into a young lady a few years ago who used that to "spice up" her personal life by using the old fashioned thigh highs and garters, but that's a personal decision.

I know what you're thinking, pantyhose are hot, and confining and.....yes I have heard all the reasons for NOT wearing them, but the plain and simple truth is that even from a distance, women look more professional, more "together", both to women and men, if they are wearing hose. Don't make it an option.

Now let's get back to an area I can speak confidently about: men! Guys there are entire books written about what you can and can't do, and should and shouldn't do.

Instead of repeating the obvious, let's go for some things we all see everyday!

1. ACCESSORIES:

Ah ha you thought only women had to accessorize, untrue, but guys have to do it better, because it is harder, here are some things to watch out for:

TIES: We all know the guy (typically a little heavier than he should be) who has the longest part of his tie; end about 3" above his belt. *Bad bad bad*! Bottom line, the Tip of the wide part of your tie should just graze the top of your belt. No one should be able to see the other part of your tie, so if it only hangs down an inch and a half, no one should be able to know. That's what tie Clips are for!

    a. And if you don't have a tie clip use money clip! It looks as good and maybe you have one around the house with not quite enough $$$ in it.

    b. If those fail, you can ALWAYS go digging through that box of jewelry gram pa left you and use cuff links! Trust me, be a little creative, but please do not use the paper clip method. I realize many of us are so economically effected now a days that, that is what we use for a money clip, but let's stop *that* habit now.

    c. Ties that are too long are just as bad, if you can tuck your tie into your belt and have it swing between your legs, this is a bad idea! Remember graze the top of your belt! We know the nursery rhyme "the bunny goes around the tree twice, down the hole and out the top, and that should give you the proper knot. Well it doesn't always work, so much like other things, if your bunny has to go around the tree 3 or 4 times, *No one should know*!

d. It has been scientifically proven that in times of increased economic stress, men make bad eating decisions, and therefore they gain weight. In other words, when guys are unemployed or unhappily employed they get fat. Women have known this for years. However, one thing that guys have to watch for, that most women don't, are "cheap pockets" betraying their weight gain! Think about it folks, how many men have you seen who are OBVIOUSLY more than 20lbs overweight and they are wearing the same pants they wore 10 lbs ago. How can you tell? Well when you are wearing black pants and from the front they can see your white pocket lining it says 2 things

1. You are not supposed to be wearing those pants at this point in your life.

2. You are not spending very much on the pants that you do buy!

You will find a night and day difference in quality and look in pants if you will just make sure that the pocket liners are the same color as the pants, trust me it will make a huge difference.

Staying with the weight situation for just a second, there are 2 things that you can do absolutely free, if you are heavier than you should be (or if your Dr. says you are, you are!).

1. If you look down at your belt and the knot in your tie disappears, you have something that needs to be dealt with. obviously what we want to do is say hey lets start eating right and exercising more and lose a few of those chins, but this is not that kind of book, instead, I want to help you deal with what you can NOW! One thing you can absolutely do now is take care of that tie/knot situation. So here is something you probably didn't think you'd see me say, but here goes – *lose the tie*! At that point it has become such a distraction (trust me folks are looking for that knot) that you not wearing a tie is a better option.

BUT you still want to look ready for the boardroom, so what do you do? Get a round collared pull over shirt that looks great and fits you well. Trust me, in this case tighter is not better, there is nothing you're showing off here. However, what do you gain by being able to lose a tie? You **gain** the function of always wearing a Sport coat. Now I live in Florida, as I write this its 98 degrees outside with 100% humidity, coats are not comfortable, I know that! But and this is where your girl friend, wife or significant other comes in to play, the proper sport coat over the proper dress Tee, can cover many sins!

2. SOMETHING you want to avoid and I see this in every man who should know better but apparently doesn't: Do not wear a collared shirt opened at the neck, such that the collar is completely flattened out and you look like you have *wings*! I don't even know how they do this. But to compound sin upon sin, these guys also typically are wearing either no T-shirt underneath, or a V neck, so you have a pasty white patch of skin poking through that looks extremely UN healthy! What should you do? See the above, but please for the love of all that is healthy, lose the look you have, it is not helping anyone! And is only hurting your look entirely

SHOES – you *need* to have at least 2 pair of shoes. One that you wear to interviews, special occasions, and one that you actually wear to work. It will pay off in the long run, without question. You are to only wear the one pair when you are attending a wedding, funeral or job interview. The other pair you wear to work. Now they should both be kept up, a regular cleaning and shining etc. But when it all comes down to it, you know you have 1 pair that you will always reach for, in times of duress.

BELTS – You need 2 black belts. Why 2? This is the same theory as above. YOU may not think folks can see it, but when the finish on your "pleather" belts starts to flake off, everyone can see it. So, buy real leather belts, and buy 2 of them. I know they cost more than you think they should, but it will always pay off. Why 2 black? Because your belt should always match your shoe colors and you notice I didn't mention brown shoes? There's a reason:

Unless you are suddenly transported back to 1972 you should not be wearing brown shoes. **Ever.**

IN SHORT:

15 things that are NEVER a good idea:

1. Underwear as outerwear. Camisoles or visible bra straps and lingerie scream nightclub, not office wear.

2. Workout gear. Save your muscle shirts and spandex for the gym. Unless you actually work in a gym, then it should a company logo.

3. Soiled stained or rumpled clothing. Neatness counts. Every now and then take your favorite white tops/shirts, and hold them up to a light, 2 things will happen:

> a. If you have ANY stains of any color they will show up.

> b. If you can tell what wattage the light is, the shirt is threadbare, and time to go.

4. Shorts. Again, unless your job description/uniform specifically highlights them, don't wear them!

5. Tattoos. Celebrities like Angelina Jolie have made tattoos seem almost proper. But many people are still put off by them. There was a time when certain jobs REQUIRED you to cover them. Since that no longer seems to be the case, think before you ink.

6. Extreme hair color. Natural looking highlights are fine, but never dye your hair blue, magenta or other colors not found in nature. Even if they are 'temporary' party spray- no's. Sometimes they do not react well when its time to wash them out.

7. Too much cologne. A strong scent is a turnoff to most people. If anyone in an elevator can tell what you're wearing, you're wearing too much. Additionally if grandma gave it to you in your stocking, wait until you visit her to wear it.

8. Long, fake or wild-colored nails. Keep your nails short and neat. Avoid nail decals, black polish or "Elvira" length nails.

9. Grungy beards. In general, most companies prefer clean-shaven men to, say, ZZ Top. If you just can't part with your facial hair, at least keep it neatly trimmed. The majority of folks over the age of 40, especially women, are still turned off by facial hair.

10. Micro-miniskirts. Your hem is below the knee never above it

11. Overly revealing attire. Too little is too much. Breasts, back and arms should be covered. In the office "Tight aint right"

12. Athletic socks with street shoes. Save that look for when you tour Europe, you'll look like every other American tourist.

13. Body piercings. Studies show that most people view body jewelry as unprofessional and that people with multiple piercings are less likely to be hired or promoted. Additionally

if you work in the food industry studies have shown that customers feel that their food is only as clean as their server.

14. Bare midriff. Again, save it for the beach. If you've read this far, you should have gotten the point.

15. Low-rise pants. "Plumber's crack" is not acceptable anywhere. Even if you're a plumber/cable guy, let's see if we can change that stereotype.

Finally, as a rule of thumb: If you have any doubt whether something you have on is appropriate -- go back and change.

Chapter 8: Start work the very first day!

Now that almost seems obvious doesn't it? You can't start before you get there, or CAN you?

1. Do you know the history of your new employee's / company / boss?

2. Have you done your homework about the situation you're walking into?

3. Do your long and short term goals align with those of your environment?

4. Are there things about you that need to change even before you get there?

If you can answer yes to any of these questions than you have undoubtedly done your homework, so really there shouldn't be any surprises that first week! But *no one* tells you everything. Regardless of how much information you may have been able to gather, there are still things that you need to learn.

So let's put you in the best frame of mind to be taught in!

1) Make sure that you START with the right (positive) attitude?

Now some office environments just do NOT want a happy go lucky "just stepped off the Positive Mental Attitude Boat" kind of guy coming in and ruining their perfectly good grumpy cube world! Believe it or not some people are miserable and like it that way. These are the same people who get mad at you for reminding them that they don't need to water the grass during a rainstorm!

Walk softly and carry a comfortable smile! Be happy but not overbearing. If you're "new friends" are tired of being around you by lunch time, then you're doing something wrong! Yes every office should be happy and humming that song. But you and I understand that some offices want it their way or the highway, and if you try and change things on day 1, you will be effectively voting yourself off the island!

2) **Although it seems tightly related to the previous idea make sure you create the right image of yourself!**
You can divide this cleanly into two different areas, **concept** and **execution**.

In this case the **concept** would be the image of you that people will arrive at by working around you. Office gossip is, unfortunately a fact of life. You however have wisely opted out of listening to, contributing to, or even paying attention to anything that looks smells or even hints of gossip, and that is a great start. Unfortunately that's all it is, a start. You can't stop what other people will say about you. What you can do, is to consider protecting your integrity with an iron clad guarantee!

If you're not doing things worth talking about, they will find someone else to open up on. The best way to make sure that this happens is by following up on what you say you will do, go the extra mile in every task that you perform and plan on exceeding everyone's expectations! Unfortunately this shouldn't be too difficult, since average has become the new outstanding! Do what you say, deliver more than you promise, in less time and under budget, and you will take away any remark or rumor that anyone should ever try to start about you. Chances are they will be so busy covering their own tracks that they won't have time to try and drag you down.

Now if Concept is what people **think** of you then **execution** must be what people see of you. If that's the conclusion that you have reached then you're right on target. **Execution** starts from the moment you step into that office for your interview, all the way to the point where you step out and retire. When they look at you what do they see?

There is an old concept, with a whole series of books behind it that says "dress for success" As true as that is, I'd like you to take it one step farther: That would be to **"dress for where you want to GO, not for where you are"** If you're in an entry level job, that's great, dress the way YOUR supervisor does. Look not one but two steps ahead of where you currently are, and that's the goal you should be aiming for!

A District Manager for a large chain of restaurants was overheard saying about one of his favorite store managers "When he comes through the door for a meeting he always looks like he has come in that day to take my job."

Having already stated that there are many, many great books on the subject I will leave you with 3 ideas, and let you flesh them out as you can:

1) Dress for the position you want, not the one you have

2) This is an office, not a nightclub.

3) Dress appropriately for the work you do.

IBM found out the hard way that requiring their copy repair people to wear neck ties was not always the smartest thing, when they were bent over the open bin with lots of rollers and cutters!

Unfortunately they also found out that allowing 'casual Friday' to become 'casual everyday' was not a really great idea as well. There was a time in this country when one person said PC some one else assumed IBM. Then the "boys in blue" started hiring young guys straight out of college who hadn't worn a suit since their first communion, and were not about to start wearing one now! IBM, thinking that they needed these young bucks started to loosen their dress code, to make them feel more at ease. You can plot the downward spiral of IBM's percentage hold of the market, by looking at the calendar of when their dress code changed. Now when someone says PC, someone else will say what a great commercial series MAC has on TV now.

Now a lot of what you see above, by the time you get into management should seem pretty obvious, but what about when your team members don't see things the way you do?

Well you have several options, let's start with the easiest and move to the most difficult. Starting with, "What is your companies view on dress code?" We start there because it's the easiest one to enforce. If your team members signed a contract (as most large companies require) that states that they will dress in a specific manner and they're not doing it, you can always dangle unemployment over their heads, until they do comply.

This is not something that I strongly suggest, instead I ask you this, and "How did your team get THIS far out of line in the first place?" I worked for a company that at the time was the largest private company doing what they did in America. Each area that they were operating in was controlled by a "Senior Manager" who received a large base salary as well as a percentage of the income generated. This Sr. Manager typically controlled anywhere between 7 and 10 offices, none of which were located any CLOSER than 3 counties away from each other.

The reason these Sr. Manager's received such a large base salary was they were spending a large percentage of it on traveling between each office each week. Typically you would see your Sr. Manager one day a week, typically on the same day every week. This Sr. Manager would then hire an Office Manager who would maintain day to day control (including the hiring and training) of his entire staff. The Office Manager would normally receive a "pretty big" base salary with a smaller percentage of the net sales. This officer manager in every case that I could find was "brought up through the business" and therefore 6 months earlier was a $10/hr "sales dog" who every X thousands of dollars in sales received a $100 bonus.

Now I am not here to tell you whether this was right or wrong, BUT when you consider that this particular Sr. Manager made a habit of hiring High School kids, then you are laying your foundation with "salesman" who don't know how to tie a tie, much less wear one. I actually had a guy who had his mom tie a tie and he left it in his locker everyday so he could wear a tie to work! So by the time these guys worked their way "to the top" they are either High School Seniors, or College Freshman (both of whom are focusing on things other than school or business), and are not used to wearing professional clothing.

I got hired by this company because I moved to this town to go to school, but already had one degree and had worked "in the real world" for 5 years and gotten burned out already. So I walked into my interview in a coat and tie. Move six months down the line and now I am "awarded an office" to manage and told I can hire my own crew and create my own rules. I was the oldest guy in the office I was selling in so the Sr. Manager thought I knew something. What I did not know was that this office was locked into a 3 year lease that was a year old, and had such poor numbers that everyone had been fired the week before.

The day I moved over there I was told that the previous manager claimed he couldn't hire anyone, and this office was across the street from a High School. Now I had only been in town 6 months so I didn't know that this was what today would be considered a D or F school. So I ran the ads, ran the interviews and could NEVER hire my "quota" of a 20 member staff. I did however exceed my "numbers" every single month for the entire time I was managing that office.

How? Well I did several things that no one else, including the Sr. Manager, had ever done, starting with, instituting a dress code. If I'm going to wear a tie, gosh darn it, so is everyone else! Also, you had to have a shirt with a collar, golf shirts need not apply. Now my first month I thought I was in danger of getting fired because my turn over was huge, but by month two when I finally started to get some folks who would "stick" I started turning out some high quality folks, and I started to do more and more with less and less.

By the time I left that company after 18 months the Sr. Manager actually offered me my own "Sr. Management" spot with a VERY large salary at the end of it. But by then I knew enough about the company and the industry to understand that its not one that I really wanted to be associated with. When I asked him why I was being offered the spot instead of the Manager that I had worked "under" initially, his answer was short and simple: "You look the part, XYZ is a good kid, but he will never look like a Senior Manager." Now I know for a fact that XYZ did eventually get his Sr. spot, but unfortunately that area was shortly absorbed by the initial Sr. Manager, who in turn made my offices dress code mandatory across all of his offices.

So yes you can hold their jobs over their heads I just don't advise it. One thing I have found that works VERY well is by combining two of my techniques into one and shooting for the same goal. I started working several years ago on what has become called "quarterly one on ones". This is a closed door meeting between me and ONE member of my team with some very specific rules and ideas. Rule #1: "what is said in that room stays in that room." Rule #2 " you must come to the meeting with 3 goals you want to accomplish in the next 6 months and 3 goals you want to accomplish within the next YEAR."

I explain that this allows me to make sure that if I agree with their goals and their timelines I can guide them properly as well as try and make sure that any projects or accomplishments that they will need to overcome will be 'thrown their way' in time for them to finish them before their next "coaching period'. During this meeting is also the time when I can bring to their attention, very tactfully, any personal issues that need to be dealt with. At a certain point those issues will rotate, if you try the 1 on 1 plan beware that you will hear, marital issues, health issues, car issues, money issues and personnel issues. They will rotate on a regular basis and you need to be careful about what you "agree/disagree" with or state that you will/wont do anything about. Having gone to the mat with an EEOC case once (and I won) I can tell you this, even if you're innocent its not any fun.

The last thing that you want to ever do to try and resolve a dress issue is to "pass it up line." Trust me, if you are in management or would ever like to be considered for management, there are certain things that you do NOT pass up line. I have one person I know who received the last available management position available that anyone would ever want (more on that later) but he was brought in at a very low pay rate, and he hasn't moved much for a very simple reason. When his Sr. Manager told him once early on, "anything you're not sure of, let me handle" and this poor Sr. Manager got more "meeting requests" from this manager, than from the entire rest of his department! Finally his Sr. said to him "what is it that you are handling?" apparently that didn't really sink in because he continued to "advertise the stupid" and so he's paying the price for doing so more than once.

Chapter 9: Staying Happy, Healthy and Wise!

You're in the industry you have always wanted to be in, working for the company you feel can give you the best return on your investment and in the job that WILL help you live the life you have always wanted to live. Most importantly you are managing the team that will lead you where you want to go!

But, before we go too far, how can we make sure that leaving where you were is the right thing to do, no one wants to be a Monday morning quarterback, and get inundated with questions or regrets? How do you make sure that you're on track for the trip that you outlined in previous chapters?

The first thing is to ask what is it that could possibly have gotten you to stay where you were.

Ask any 10 folks and you will get 10 *different* ways to say MONEY. The worst part of course is that they are all kidding themselves. Money will *only* placate you for so long, and then, sooner rather than later you will find yourself at your desk again, or out in the shop again, wondering about what *could* have happened, if only... You will "if only" yourself to death.

So, assuming that more money would not have made a big enough difference for you to stay and statistics agree that money *is* just a short term solution one of 2 things has happened to you:

1) You forgot what YOU wanted out of that job in the first place.

This typically will happen if you start with a company because they had something new to teach you in the way of technical expertise and either, you weren't excited by what you learned or, they never really got around to making your education their priority!

So if *that* was the case, ask yourself a few more tough questions:

a. *What* was that subject? What was it that they offered that really interested you? Was it something that *you* wanted to learn that would then help your job? Or was it just something that you had to have for your job?

b. Does it still interest you? If this was a subject that you wanted to learn that would also help in your job is it something that you still want to learn? If so why? If not why not? More importantly, would developing that skill help you in what you want to do *now*?

You would be amazed at *how many* folks have "lost their way" on the track to success, just because they were moving so fast, they forgot to step back and appreciate what they were learning! Or worse yet, they forgot that they were learning, and started gathering a small, or rather large resentment towards those around them! Maybe it's time to step back, look at what you _are_ doing, compare it to what you _want_ to do, and start working towards _that_ instead!

2) Did you feel that this company had a faster fast track than any one else out there who was hiring at the time? Sometimes a certain company gets a reputation, in the industry, as becoming the "it "place to be!

You know, if you want that Microsoft Elevator Operator Certification THAT there is ONLY one place to be so that you become certified. So you go and sign up, and realize that the market has changed, the job and industry that you thought you wanted has changed, now this company churns out DOZENS of elevator operators every year, only to discover then that the rest of the industry has turned to escalators!

3) Ask yourself if the skill set that you thought you wanted only lead to an early and **un**wanted retirement? OR are you just now determining that THIS is the time to start learning something new!

In the worst case scenario of course, did you just need a job? Maybe you were in a situation where in order to get a job _any_ job that you would need a certain minimum educational skill in order to qualify. Once again, does that _still_ apply to your _new_ career alternative? Sometimes you get _so_ caught up/bored in the day to day that you have _lost_ your way!

If this really does describe you, than there is more going on here than I can cover in just a limited number of pages, but I will say that you are NOW at a point in your life where change is now a must.

It may be that you need to change in order to help you, or change to help your family or perhaps just change to be friendlier in what you do and say so that more ideas will come your way.

We can help you work on finding what you want, but only if <u>you</u> determine that you are uncomfortable enough in your life to actually <u>do</u> something about it!

Let's say you actually get your foot into the door, now what? Your **big** goal was to get that job, now you have it now you need to make your next set of goals:

"But J I worked so hard to get this job, can't I just sit back and enjoy it for a while? Don't I get a break? "No, you don't have time for breaks, you don't have time to rest you don't really even have time to look around. But do take advantage of those 1st 30 days, during which no one really expects much out of you anyway, so NOW is the time to really pour it on.

First, make sure that you complete every assignment you get, complete to your utmost and highest, ability. Make the MOST out of every meeting you attend (and there will be a lot of them). Take notes, make sure you become known, but <u>be quiet</u>.

Now there is something that sounds contradictory right? WRONG. As SOON as you sit down, and before the meeting actually starts, introduce yourself around (remember names, <u>write them down</u>), find a way to work in titles and or responsibilities, but do so tactfully, you don't want to walk up to your CEO and go "Hi! What do *you* do around this joint?"

So make your notes, make them clear, and refer to them often; <u>but</u> during the meeting itself you might want to measure your thoughts carefully. Obviously if you are asked a direct question you will need to answer it as directly and as honestly as possible but also realize you have 2 ears and 1 mouth for a <u>very</u> important reason.

A wise man once told me that he went to a millionaire and asked "sir what can I do to place me on the path to earning a million dollars?" Well the millionaire took a deep breath and let it out very slowly. When he had composed himself he said, "You know son the biggest issue that most folks have is saying too much, too soon or when it has no FIT in the conversation."

The <u>best</u> thing you can do for yourself is this, if a thought comes to your mind, you hold onto it, and slowly count to 10. When you get to 10, look at the current state of the conversation, and compare the observation that you would like to make. The majority of the time what you will find is that the conversation will have moved on beyond your comment and it will no longer be relevant. Sometimes you will find that someone else has made your comment, albeit perhaps slightly differently than you would have, but still the same information. very rarely you will find that your comment is still relevant, when that actually does occur, choose your words carefully and explain your comment and how to process your information exactly.

I used to work in a 3 story building, on the floor below mine, everyone made more money than I did, but was in my same range. Elsewhere on MY floor there were a hundred other folks, some making more some making less. On the floor immediately above ours was the alphabet soup crowd. You know, these are all the folks (and their secretaries) who have those letters after their names "CEO, CIO, CFO etc"

My manager of the time reminded us that if we worked in that building long enough we would find ourselves in the elevator with one of these folks and THEY had a huge advantage. See everyone in MY pay grade was required to wear a badge with our department name and our first name on it. So it was nothing for the CIO to look over and go "So Jerome, Tell me about the latest project you're working on.

The advantage was theirs, because you didn't know WHO this person was, if they rated any information, if telling them was a confidentiality conflict etc. So she suggested that we prepare an "elevator speech"

An elevator speech is a 30 second to 1 minute answer of whom you are and what you're working on, and why **that** should justify your continued employment there! As an example if you do not know who is asking the question and they say, "So John (reading your company ID) what are you fellows in IS working on now?" Your answer should be fairly straightforward and simple, <u>without</u> sounding as though you're trying to brush him off. Because remember you don't even know who *he* is (Most executives don't wear company IDs) "Well sir as a Team Lead I see it as my primary focus to work with my team mates and get them promoted as quickly as they can be to positions where their skills are best utilized, all while making sure my manager receives proper credit"

You have just told Mr. 100K/yr that you are a team player who is more concerned with the folks he manages and the folks who manage HIM than you are yourself!

Now let's say that this person is someone that you know, if not personally, at least you know that he is the chief of your area, someone who really HAS a pretty good idea of what your working on. Choose one thing that you are most knowledgeable about, that you know is working and tell them about that! "So John what's the Ancillary App team lead focused on today?"

"Well Sir as you may be aware we have isolated two rather large areas of data leak in our XYZ system and we're working with the vendor to patch that, alternatively Kathy is working with our integration team to develop a home grown solution that we would own from the ground up."

It's not too complex, but you've told him, that if the vendor can't fix it **you** can and best of all YOUR Company will OWN the solution. Executives like home grown solutions that don't take an entire department to implement or manage. Whatever you choose, be **honest** and **succinct**.

Chances are, they are just being polite passing the time in an enclosed space. Don't make yourself *too* big or *too* important and worse yet, don't elaborate. When your manager finds out about the conversation (and they will) you don't want them coming to you with the question "So I heard you were working on a cold fusion reactor at your desk, when can I see the prototype?

Now your conversation as a Manager is going to be of a completely different nature. Why? Because chances are you are already a point of conversation in his world at some point. This of course is why you rarely find managers using elevators. But realize that when a Sr. Manager asks one of his managers a question in the hall, chances are he knows the answer already, or has an idea of what the answer should be, based on something that was said by someone, somewhere else in his realm.

What's this mean for you? As a manager do not lie, cheat, steal, elaborate or fabricate anything that you ever tell anyone who gets paid more than you, or knows someone who gets paid more than you do. Remember I mentioned that the alphabet soup crowd and their secretaries worked above me? Well somewhere along the way I must have helped one of these "administrative assistants" at some point because she knows me by name and takes every possible opportunity to strike up a conversation with me.

Every time I saw her I would ask someone on my team (who made it their business to KNOW everything about everyone) who she was and why I should care. Because I have no memory, I am reminded that she is the Sr. VP of XYZ's administrative assistant. My knowing she was someone important, yet not knowing exactly who I am talking to requires me to come up with a very generic sounding idea of some project I'm working on. Because, of course, she eats with everyone else's secretaries and what I say has the chance of being repeated 10 times over in one day.

My next rule of management is very important for folks wanting to BE in management: Do *not* let your boss get surprised! Everyone has someone up stream from them that ignores 99% of their emails, and that's o.k. as long as you have the paper trail that you sent it. If it is something as big as a career changing event then I would follow up a day or 2 later with a personal visit to the manager (if he hasn't heard it from you yet) letting him know what the issue is and that the vendor *is* working on it. However, many vendor solutions cost, so he needs to be aware of that. Even if you're team is able to generate a home grown solution your home grown solution will cost, so you're senior managers will need to know how they compare in cost and ease of implementation and cost of maintenance.

Most people hate to have to "toadie" (not my term) up to someone who gets paid more than they do. However I can not tell you how often I have seen a career ended because a Sr. Manager was caught off guard, by something that was happening in their own team. Rarely will you see, as demonstrated on TV , a Sr. Manager fire someone on the spot, although that is always an available option, but I personally have observed several careers put on hold for between 6 months to two years, while someone "learned a lesson" for a mistake that was made. You don't want your career to be caught in that kind of trap.

There are some Sr. Managers who will call a "one on one" meeting with their managers every week, and in those meetings you are usually given free reign to say and do what you need to say and do. However if your Sr. is of a particular personality type, who wants to get it done and get it done now, you will need to make sure that you put some specific information in front of that Sr. in between these meetings. Therefore you must find the most effective way to do that every single time you have the opportunity. I was the most frustrated person in the company because I had one VP who NEVER seemed to answer my emails until so much time had passed as it was no longer relevant. Then I found out that *this* person filtered all his emails, and only read them once a week.

Rather than go stand on his desk and explain how outrageously ridiculous I thought this was (and still do), I instead found out how else I could talk to him. Well it turned out that at X:45 every day he walked down the back stairs of the building so he could walk to the gym. I didn't want to join a gym, but amazingly enough this VP and I found ourselves on those backstairs at least one day a week, and I had his undivided attention, during THAT few minute walk.

Chapter 10: How to get WHAT and WHERE you want, once you're IN the office!

You're **IN**. You have the right job with the right company; you're leading the right TEAM and you're being led by the right person! – Now WHAT?

Obviously you will need to give yourself some time to get acclimated, but it is NEVER too early to start moving in the direction that you want. I'm confident that ANYONE with the skill set to perform their job competently, can then use the tools I'm about to show you, and find themselves in a promotion position not once. But twice a year!

The best part about these tools is the best time and the easiest time to put them into place is anytime you come into a new area/job/position etc. People don't know exactly what to expect of you, so if you create the impression that you want them to have, you are creating a set of "fans" for yourself and your career. Not to mention that as a "new manager" your team is going to compare you (positively or negatively) to the person who sat in that chair last.

Start early, stay late and work the entire time your in the office!

I know this sound like a no brainier right? But are you currently doing it where you are now? Probably not, we all need a "little break every now and then right?" After all you worked really hard on getting that automatic toilet flushing campaign up and running, you NEED a breather. Yes, as soon as your CIO takes a breather you can too, until then, get to work!

Now if you are the office gossip and suddenly you come to work Monday morning and start acting differently, folks are going to think that either you're under disciplinary action, or they are waiting for "the other shoe to drop." So if you are currently in that position, you can still implement these ideas and reap their rewards, you just may want to start more slowly and slightly more discreetly! By the way if you are the office gossip, chances are you are reading this to learn how to get into management. If that is your situation my first suggestion is, **stop being the office gossip**. No one trusts you and they never will.

Remember earlier, Start early stay late? I was serious about that. If you do this several things will happen:

1) You will start you see just exactly who the 'workers' are. Typically folks won't show up at 6:30 just so they have more time to cruise the internet. Although I'm sure that if you speak to enough managers, you will find enough people who can find an example of exactly that.
2) You will start to be seen by the folks that matter. The CIO, the owner of the company, your Sr. Manager. All these people, who are in a position to help your career, will start to *see* you, and noting what time you come in, and go home, will start to take a very positive notice of you.

3) Lastly, and this is something you have to guard against, you will also start to see the folks who arrive late and leave early.

Every company has those few folks who show up just at the last minute, and then 'slipping out' just as early as they can! My pet peeve was the folks who slide in at just the last minute, sit down at their desk, login, and then go get their coffee. Bring it back set it down, open up their email then go get their breakfast. They have been on campus 45 minutes, performed 2 work related tasks and gotten their coffee, donuts and breakfast! We actually had an employee who had convinced her boss to allow her to arrive at 4am so that she could leave right after lunch! Who in the world is going to be there to verify a 4 am schedule? No one that I know who works in most industries, but there also wasn't anyone who could question her on it. So when you start seeing these things, the hard part of your job is to stay focused on you. It will catch up to them, I promise bad behavior is eventually caught, and long patterns of it, usually invite a request to find employment elsewhere.

Try NOT to get involved in the office politics!

The last part of my opening statement, work the entire time that you are in the office! Look, I know the Internet is a fascinating place, you can find out about more strange things than you ever knew existed, but if you're serious about what you want, get a broadband connection at your house and leave the cruising for home! By now, having gone through steps 1, 2 and 3, you have the bosses' attention. If you are out performing and out producing every other manager in the company that's a great place to be, however you DON'T want his attention focused on you if you're watching the Southeastern TRI-Annual corn shuckers Winter Olympics on StupidVideos.com!

Most managers *know* the office scoop of whom the talkers are and who is producing results. If you're NEW your not going to be IN that group, do everything you can NOT to be in that group. If a co worker 'drops' by your desk and its not lunch time, let them know that whatever it is that your working on is very important, but as soon as you get done, (maybe find out where they will be at lunch) you'll get right back to them. Make it polite, but make it known that you're not the one to go to with the latest office gossip or your working on something special for the boss. Eventually they will get the hint, and you'll get the time that you need to do the work that you're being paid for. Regardless of how the week is going, if YOU start getting more done, you'll start having more and better assignments handed down from up above and that's a good thing!

Remember my one on one's? Well I worked for a company that had a smoking area, and of course at that time, smoking was the one thing that bound together dozens of folks who wouldn't even look in each others directions if they saw them in the hall. But when they needed nicotine you could be their best friend. I can't tell you how often I had to "advise" my team members to avoid that area. I had some folks who got down right **nasty** if they couldn't smoke, yet here I was trying to convince them to stay away from the one area where they could "relax" during the day.

This was not because I really cared about their health, it wasn't really even because smelling like an ashtray was a very unprofessional thing to do. It was because in that area there was more gossip, innuendo and hearsay occurring than anywhere else in the company. I would give the example, that if I listened to office opinion I would be packing my desk up on a regular basis, sometimes because I was about "to get the axe" and sometimes because I was getting moved to a VP position.

Yet most people who spent their time in that area were very poor filters of information. They would hear something and then react to it. Instead of trying to verify or validate or better yet, consider the source. No instead they would run like Chicken Little screaming that the stocks are falling.

So, use that time to dispense "suggestions" for what may or may not be something good or bad to their career. Nine times out of ten the people in the position to make a difference in your career are watching the people who run around repeating things that they shouldn't and creating a mental list. On that list are all the names and reasons on why one person or another is not going to get promoted next year.

Remember earlier when I said stay away from office politics? Well now I'm going to take that one step farther and that is, stay away from Politics of any kind. There are whole lists of subjects that almost any women's magazine worth their ink will run about once a year, and it starts with "The subjects to Avoid during your first date." Well I want to take it one step farther and say that you need to clip these subjects and post them inside your briefcase. If you think they are a bad idea on a date they are a **nightmare** when used in the office.

If you do not yet know your HR officer, but really want to, start a conversation in the office one day that revolves around sex, drugs, religion, health care, political affiliation etc. These are HIGHLY explosive subjects that many people feel very deeply about and take their opinions very seriously and hold very dearly.

Finally if you want to see something blow up in your face tell a "joke" about any of those subjects, in your office at anytime of the day or night, to anyone be they at your level, a VP or a member of housekeeping. Very quickly you will find yourself in front of some member of management, hopefully one you KNOW, so that you only get a written reprimand and not a termination slip.

Humor is great, if you want to expose your friends at work to it, take them to Bonkers on Friday night, but do NOT bring Bonkers or your favorite episode of the Simpson's in with you to work on Monday morning!

Not only is this a nightmare for employees but if you are a member of management it is doubly dangerous for you for several reasons, not the least of which is that your company is expecting you to police this type of activity, and then hand out the discipline when and if it comes to that.

Let me give you the most ridiculous experience I have EVER seen and I will do my best to keep this as generic as I possibly can.

I worked in a mid level position in a company that valued its employees not at all. As a matter of fact during my training period I asked a manager what their turn over was and he admitted it was 100% every 12 months. For those that don't understand, due to the size of this company it meant that they trained and retrained 500 people every single year. While I was there I actually met several folks who were very talented. I moved out and up the next year (hey I was one of the 500), and kept in contact with those folks that I knew could do better.

So I soon found myself advising management on who to hire and how to interview and in doing so brought over about 5 folks from that previous company. However there was this one guy, I'll call him John, which I just could never get in the door. I tried several different positions over several different years. Just changing companies would have given John a 30% raise. That's good money no matter who you are.

Finally I was in a situation where I had almost complete autonomy in hiring and training and I still couldn't get John hired. I only had to get one other person to agree with me, and for some reason other people kept getting hired into the positions. So finally I called his wife told her what to tell him and how to get him the job. He came in, got the job, everything seemed fine.

Now one thing I have neglected, because it didn't matter to me, was this gentleman was handicapped. You wouldn't know unless he told you, but as soon as upper management found out about him we started getting all kinds of commendations from everyone about how great it is we opened up our teams to ...blah blah blah. Again I didn't care I couldn't figure out why anyone else did.

Well over the next several months I started noticing some behaviors that were 100% off target with what I thought I knew about this guy. But I'm the guy who can teach anyone anything, so I knew it could be fixed. So I spent several months working with him, and several months later it just didn't seem to be working. So then I had to involve my boss.

When it got to that level John decided that OK, maybe there was something to be said and so he promised things would get better. Well we hired someone else in from another team and I got bogged down bringing that person up to speed and so I left John to his own devices. Then I started to notice that goals were not being achieved and we were starting to get late notices from some of our partners. After some paper tracking I realized that once again I was back to John.

So this time I started with my boss, since his conversation had been so much more effective than mine. That's where I was informed that John was apparently 'afraid of me' and feeling threatened. Now I am in now way a large guy, and so when I have to look UP at anyone, I find it rather amusing that I was considered threatening, but no I was told, **this** was NOT funny. Now all disciplinary conversations were to be left to my boss. Ok I washed MY hands of the whole thing.

Then I got the text message after I left one night that John had "left the building" and would not be back on premises. To make a **ridiculously** long story a tad shorter, it turns out that while John was telling management he was afraid of me he was physically intimidating anyone in his path, after I left the premises.

Once that he no longer worked for the corporation he approached "Dewey, Cheatham and Howe, Attorneys at Law" to see how much money he could get. I don't know all the details, but common theory held that in situations like this employees were offered 2 weeks salary and asked to go away. Apparently that was not sufficient because John pursued this for many months, even past the point of being told by several governing bodies that he had no case, and after more than a year, during which several people were very much in fear of losing their jobs, it was ended in a court telling him he had no case.

Now I'm not going to go into how many dumb moves were made in this whole scenario. I will say that as his supervisor, if I had known several things about his home life that I knew AFTER he was hired, I never would have hired him. But once he HAD the job, I also was told that several employees had a prank pulled on **them** by John, about his handicap. Now this would not have been so odd, other than part of johns accusation was that his handicap was being held against him.

Proof that amazing things can come from ridiculous situations. Also, proof that even if you think its funny there is at least one person who won't, and that one person could make it very uncomfortable for the rest of the staff. That unfortunately is a commentary on our society that falls outside the scope of this book.

Chapter 11: Orientation, once you get to your Office, then what?!

From Webster.Com:

Main Entry: **ori·en·ta·tion** Function: *noun* Date: 1839

1 a : the act or process of orienting or of being oriented **b :** the state of being oriented; *broadly* **:** arrangement, alignment
2 a : a usually general or lasting direction of thought, inclination, or interest **b :** a person's self-identification as heterosexual, homosexual, or bisexual <sexual orientation>
3 : change of position by organs, organelles, or organisms in response to external stimulus

Now I could just go ahead and ASK which of those definitions you think would be more appropriate for a business discussion, but if you manage your own business or are deeply involved in managing the company you're in, you already noticed one thing about the above definition. Any one of those definitions could be relating to business and professional attitude. But let's focus on just one group of terms, those that are described under definition #2 – a direction of **thought**.

So, now you're working for the company you want, working in the career you want, managing the team you want. How do you keep moving ahead, quickly, effectively, and in a direction similar to that of your superiors? I believe that the following tools can help you do exactly *that*!

1) Be FUTURE oriented in your life and your work!

Don't worry about the history of the team, its members or how it played out in the companies past. If you find out that the folks who are on your new team are there because the company can't afford to fire them, but wants to put them somewhere where they won't hurt anything, that's the past! Choose not to participate in it! Do not get involved in discussions about "the good old days" or "remember when's." Those are all things that have happened and that you have no control over so don't waste time or attention by focusing another minute in their direction.

Instead always look ahead. Look "down the road" in your life both at work and at home, because at ANY moment they can become permanently intertwined, and THAT you should avoid. But stop doing what your doing and consider for a moment exactly WHAT long term effects your project or instructions could have on, this project, this team or this organization 6 months, 1 year and 5 years from now. You're in a position of leadership, this is now the opportunity that you have needed to get others involved IN the company's decisions. Show them what the end goals are, and the best ways that they can reach and contribute to them. People want to be contributors to the future, now is your chance to let it show.

Create a **long** term vision, both in yourself and in your team! Share this vision with your team. If you can, also share some of the thinking behind what Sr. Management has up their sleeves when they move an entire division, or when they talk about outsourcing departments. If you give your team members some ideas or reasons to focus on, then their options for helping to make it happen will go straight up. Plus you have taken some of the air out of the tires of some of those who just gravitate towards creating a little more stress in their lives. It is very important for your team members to know **where** they are going, but almost as important, is WHY they are working so hard to get the company there!

Use this time and this information to help your team members develop *long term visions* for their own careers. Many folks, unless they are guided through the process will never give their all, unless you allow them to get involved in the WHY of the dream. This is **your** opportunity to not only spread the work, but spread the load as well. You do that by finding out "what's next" and infusing those ideas into the minds of some of your brightest individuals. Once inspired, they can help motivate the rest.

Always remember the best way to predict the Future is to help **create** the Future. If your team is aware of what needs to get done, and why it needs to get done, they will be willing to help more and more, and <u>do</u> more and more things that are outside of their comfort zones, just so that they can contribute to their own future!

2) Be GOAL oriented in everything that you do.

This one is such a simple concept that I almost don't want to take the time to explain it. But unfortunately if you don't take the time to explain it, or to understand it, you are setting yourself up to fail. A wise man once asked a crowd of people if they knew which way a motorcycle went. Everyone of course looked for the "trick" to the question, but in reality it was a very simple question. A motorcycle rider is the one who finally came up with the right answer "The motorcycle goes wherever you are looking." That's the same as it is with people. You will end up wherever it is that you are focused,

Unfortunately it has been proven time and time again that the average worker in America will spend more time planning his two weeks vacation in the Summer than he will planning out the future of his career. We are not taught goal-setting in college, so most folks just never learn it. If they did somehow pick up the skill set they may apply it once even twice in their life, and then after that it's the same as it always has been; moving from point to point in their Jobs, never looking out and beyond where they are, to make sure that they are even on the career path.

A plane flying from Chicago to L.A. will spend over 90% of its time heading in a direction other than west which is why a plane has an automatic transponder that will send out a signal every 20 miles and says; "I'm here, this is where I'm going, am I on the right track?" It will then receive back a course correction and put the plane back on the right course. Maybe it was snow, or rain, or just the wind that blew it off course ever so slightly. But on a flight from Chicago to L.A, a deviation of just 2 degrees will have you sailing in the ocean in a matter of hours. Instead a series of tiny course corrections will keep you on the straight path as much as you need to be in order to reach your goals. How much more important is your career than a plane ride across country. So don't fly off course, check in with someone who has been where you are headed, let them help you. In everything you do, keep your end goal, your results, in front of you!

Now what happens if you take charge of a team that has been together for quite some time, and they neither want nor are they interested in their own goals or the future or vision of the company? Replace them. Yes I know that this sounds rather cavalier, but honestly there are very few people in any company that are truly irreplaceable. Now obviously you don't want to, I hope, walk through the area and start wholesale terminations, but you need to find your weakest link, typically they have the most to say about nothing, keep an eye on them, document their actions and then find a way to help them find another career in another company.

Please note, document their issues and then work on the termination. In today's litigious environment the last thing you want to do is fire someone "because." Dewey, Cheatham and Howe ESQ.

will be on your doorstep in a heartbeat, and that is something you don't want to have to deal with. Often by selecting the 'weakest link' early on in your leadership you will generate a sense of "fear" which may not be the best way to lead, but it is a great way to get folks to pay attention to who you are, and what you believe.

Occasionally you may find yourself in a situation where you have been promoted to manage a team that you were just a working member of the day before. Now this is not a good practice, but it does happen, because most folks are also not setting up a proper line of ascension in their area. Why is this problem? Well Monday you were sharing shooters at Happy hour, and tomorrow you are managing those same guys you were tearing management down with last week. This often leads to a long haul to the top of a leadership and respect hill.

So how do you make that transition? Your best method is to surround yourself with some "muscle" as quickly as you can. Muscle is a way to label those folks who will give you blind allegiance to you, they agree with your thoughts and your vision and they will back you up, in anything you say and do. Why do you need this muscle? Because you are going to have to start making some very tough decisions and those guys you were sharing wings with last week, will find it easier to hear it from someone they don't know than someone they do know. Believe it or not at 5'-6" I was actually the "muscle" for one of my managers in one job. Unfortunately for me, what that led to was me gaining a reputation for being a "hard case" so when the job came up that I would be perfect for, it took several months and a few promises from managers I served with to convince our Sr. Managers that, that was just a role I was playing, and in reality I was something quite different than what they had spent the last several years watching me do.

Now you find these folks who will surround you and swear their "allegiance to you." I am not saying find those slobbering zombies who will throw themselves in traffic if you ask them. Typically your muscle will be folks who actually could have had your job, but for one small thing. For example the team I was on when I was "muscle" for the manager, we started the same week, we had similar backgrounds and our abilities almost matched 100%. So why did she get the management job and I didn't? Well 3 months after I started I made a mistake, it could have been a huge mistake, and on paper it was a terminable offense. I didn't get fired because the "reason" I gave for making the excuse was a real tear jerker (details of this are just not relevant). So I kept my job, but in the eyes of those who held "my career" I was now six months behind this other person. That's how long they "unofficially" placed me on a promotion freeze. Now don't get me wrong I was getting raises at the top percentage available, because they did not want to lose me, but I also was completely **un promotable** for six months. That was to be my punishment. This was confirmed for me when the Sr. manager left a few years later.

Many people, me included in other situations, would have quit in a huff and taken my talents elsewhere. But I didn't, I stayed. Why? Because the three of us (we were all hired within a week of each other) got together at lunch one day and decided that if one of us got promoted to a certain point, the other two would become their support team. Because we all had a joint vision that together we could turn a very low end department into a dynamic powerhouse. Within three years we did exactly that. We were able to transform our department into the most efficient, most productive and well loved department in an entire corporation.

That is the kind of muscle you need. Why? Because as a management team with a shared vision of what the department could become we considered our end result in every decision we made. This included the hiring, firing and training of new team members. In a single month we were able to slim down the "training" in this department of new employees from 14 days to 3. Now understand that once someone was hired by the company they would spend between two and ten days in mandatory orientation training. The length of time was determined by the specialization of their skills. Meaning that the more unique their skill set the longer it took to get a new employee from **zero** to productive. All the while he is sucking the monetary resources out of your budget.

In the old model he would then spend another ten days in "on the job" training in the department itself. The challenge was that the Ten days was actually an endurance test more than anything else, as this "training" was downright painful to endure! So we replaced the trainer, burned the training documentation and boiled it down to exactly what was vital to know to do their job. Our very first "guinea pig" to train under this method was someone who was **so** cocky that during his interview when he heard about a 10 day training period, he said he could do it in three. So that was who we used our new theory on. telling him that we knew our stuff was good so obviously if he wasn't ready in three days it must be him, and since the probation period was 90 days...

    Again, so many folks get confused by my using of the term "muscle" but that was part of it as well. Our Sr. Manager was very good at what she did, and she used her "muscle" as her heart and her head. When something came up that needed the "people "touch, she went to my partner. If she needed something that she didn't want to consider the human element she came to me, it was a great balance.

    Unfortunately when she left and it was time to promote, I of course was 6 months behind on the timeline so the "heart" got the promotion, which was fine, since he was smart enough to make sure I was assigned to his team. Again he and I had a good run together, then he got moved to another team, and I didn't go. We'll tell the rest of that story in another book.

    I will say that his replacement (I didn't apply) came in with **no** muscle that he could trust and thus spent a full year being manipulated by various parts of his team, only to finally understand that the only team in the department that was consistently productive and consistently at peace, was the one I lead.

But I think that by now you have a clearer idea of what kind of muscle you need and how you should be using it. This of course is only important if you want **your** job to be easy, your team to be productive and your star to outshine everyone else's.

Chapter 12: 21 Steps to Success in Management.

1) Give more than what's expected

Have I mentioned this one before? Wow, think that might mean it's important?

Drive through almost any fast food franchise in your area, do you get the same chance that I do to play that wonderful new game that's sweeping the nation? You know "guess what's IN the bag!" Sometimes you really begin to wonder if perhaps there is a box between you and the one that sends your voice back to the drive through order taker, you know a box that changes your voice from English to something akin to ESPERANTO? It's not bad enough that you need to repeat yourself 10 – 12 times, but then what they repeat back NEVER matches what's on the little screen in front of you, and watch out for those times when they say "Oh I'll fix it when you get here" Trust me, it WON'T get fixed, at least not in any way that even resembles what your order should have been.

Why is that? Well it's the same reason behind why America is no longer the strongest economic empire on the planet. **Mediocrity has become acceptable**. It's not right it just IS. So if you do, just a little extra, 5 to 10% extra, you will stand out like you're painted in gold with lasers shooting from your eyes. That would be a good thing! Do a little, gain a lot of recognition!

Now how do you verify that the "extra" that you're doing is being recognized and that your NOT being taken for granted? You can't, You won't, and you will. Now, back away from the edge, this does NOT mean that this is a worthless endeavor. By performing just a little more than your asked, a little more than is expected you will start doing several things. First you will start building "credit" up in areas that you can't see yet.

One thing you have to understand is that someone is ALWAYS watching you. I'm not talking about those who are looking to get your job. I'm talking about people that you don't see, haven't considered who one day could have a huge impact on your career.

I spent a decade consulting with a commercial bank, starting in the lowest position that would support me and moving rather quickly into a situation where I was making more money than I had ever earned. The entire time I was working and doing things that were somewhat outside the norm for their consultants. What we were doing was providing some personal same day service that I would expect from a bank that was going to see several million of *my* dollars move through them every year. Unfortunately it seemed to strike most of them as a brand new idea!

During one of their "award trips" I was set next to an elderly gentleman who seemed very quiet and reserved, when compared to the rest of the "yahoos." Over the salads we started to develop a conversation and found a few interesting similarities that wouldn't have come to either of us, without this time. After the trip, we both went back to our separate states and continued our consulting. What I didn't know was that over the next several months he would spend a few minutes every week talking with the "accounts managers" who were handling my customers, and he started discovering some VERY strong similarities in how we handled things.

Over the next year I "received" several interesting leads that came into the main bank, but were asking for my team specifically. Although it was a little unusual I didn't think about it to hard, but I really enjoyed the huge dollars that it started to generate in my life. Unfortunately the next time I saw him, was a few years later, he had finally succumbed to an illness he had been concealing for quite some time, and so I had sent him some information "outside " normal channels and he wanted to thank me for it. However it was me who ended up thanking him as I discovered shortly after we started talking every single one of those leads had come from he or his partner. They appreciated meeting my wife and I and watching us work, and the extra efforts we exhibited, and so whenever something came up that would have caused a "conflict" personally, they would send them in my direction.

So going a little farther than was the norm, **not** shouting it from the rooftops and continuing to make sure that my folks were taken care of, I was able to generate several hundred thousand dollars in business all generated through a relationship that I didn't realize was as important as it turned out to be.

Finally here is a situation about not accepting a job I could have learned in six months. The person, who was finally hired into that area, was part of that team when I interviewed for the position. She had a good working relationship with my team at the time and great work ethics. Apparently she found out that during the "interview" after I turned down the spot, I was asked who I would suggest could excel. Hers was the only name I thought was qualified, she felt as though she owed me for her job. Since then, that relationship has turned into my team being able to gather information from her team much faster and more efficiently than any other team in the company!

Again, you don't know what you don't know. And you don't know who's watching you at any one time, and may be "keeping track" of your accomplishments. Those same folks can come through for your when you least expect it.

2) Awareness – be aware of what you believe

Believe in? Wait I thought this was a book about Management techniques? It is, and if you climb down out of the tree for a second you'll start to understand. But if you need the "quick fix" understand this, during your first year in management of any large corporation what you think, feel and believe will be tested at every turn. So if your not secure you're going to find things getting very rough very quickly!

The subject of Awareness has been covered elsewhere, but to add just a few ideas on to what we've already talked about, have you ever been operating with an awareness about something that just wasn't true? For example, many of us were raised with the belief that Darwin, of Evolution fame, made the statement that "Only the Strong shall survive." Well I have looked through his entire collection of writings and that statement never appears anywhere! He **did** say, however, that *"The species MOST adaptable to change would survive anything."* Similar but not exactly the same, and if you look into what they mean, they are two DRAMATICALLY different statements!

In your own life, are you seeing what's really in your OWN belief window? Are you able to see the reality of what you believe? My dad always said "Son, if you want to be President of the United States one day, you can be." But do you know what it takes to become the president? More importantly are you doing the things that you need to do, in order to become President? If not then maybe you're belief window isn't quite clean enough, and your own view of what you want and what you'll have to do to get there is slightly skewed.

Now when you apply that to being or becoming the best manager that your company has ever seen, you are going to find that the majority of the things that you think about your situation are in fact not true.

For example, there is a "standards" association, related with a company I worked with once called ITL. Without getting too bogged down, ITL was a system of "best practices" established for an industry. The company I was with required all of their managers to attend classes, read books and obtain certifications in all things ITL. These new managers would then return from their training all fresh faced and scrubbed with a whole notebook full of great ideas. After all these are required by their company, they must want us to implement them right?

What then happens is that you spend the next 90 days laying out a 5 year plan on how to implement these ideas to streamline your department, increase productivity and boost your value to the bottom line by leaps and bounds!

They then spend the next 90 days beating their head against one wall or another, trying to get past step 2 of their 5 year plan! They have these grandiose ideas that **must** be supported by the organization. But they keep encountering problems implementing them, no matter where they turn or what they do.

Their third 90 day's reality starts to dawn upon them so that they start to replay and rewrite their 5 year plan, instead making a series of 1 year plans 5 years out. They are also developing ways to try and work around some of the walls that they ran into the first two times.

The final 90 days (of year one) they come to the complete realization that these "standards" are called best practices because given an unlimited budget with an infinitely talented staff they could start to put these things into place. But because they have a very small (and shrinking) budget and they are required to work from the talent that they are able to "recruit" into their organization. They must then start trying to "cobble" together something resembling a team.

The first 90 days of the next year, they then watch the newest set of managers coming back from their ITL certifications all full of fire and desire and hoping that perhaps one of them will come ask for advice so that they can pull back the curtain and demonstrate the reality of what's actually happening. Unfortunately the new folks don't, after all they have all the answers right?

3) Communication and Presentation Mastery

Most people do **not** understand what that idea means, and even once they do start to have an idea, they still are unsure as to what the answer could be. But what we are leading to is this: The number **one** conflict in business today is caused by miscommunication. Why miscommunication? Even with a free public education, Americans are very poor communicators. English is one of the most difficult languages on the planet because we have so many words for the same thought or idea! Ancient Greeks had it easy, what they said was exactly the thought that they were thinking! But think about it, a presentation could be something as big and extravagant as a speech before the shareholders, or the elevator speech that lasts less than 30 seconds. In a single week you will make hundreds if not thousands of presentations, and good or bad, you are being judged on every single one of them. Every time you call a client, have a meeting with your boss, or write an email, someone is judging your presentation!

There was one company that I worked for where the administration was so tight I would spend 45 minutes writing, proofing and changing a single email. All because I knew that my superiors would read and critique it, whether I heard anything more about it or not!

Join Toastmasters; get good at presenting both yourself and your ideas! More importantly encourage your team to do the same. They are making almost as many presentations as you are, to the same people.

I once managed a team for a company; this team had been a team for more years than I even wanted to think about. Yet no one, had ever taught them about communication or presentations. By the end of my first month managing this team, I had redlined so many emails that had been sent out by this team that some of them got scared to push send. I will admit that it did get wearing for them to have me proofread every thing they wanted to send. But after a fairly short period of time, this same team was able to not only send out communications that could surpass anything written by the Sr. Management, but they were also able to start reading the truth in what they received.

Please, do not think that I'm suggesting that you should now assume the role of English teacher to your team of 40 year old employees, what I am suggesting is that if you want your information to be read, if you want to get your point across, you have to put it in a format that the reader understands.

For example, and I believe I have mentioned this, I once had a Sr. VP who would look at an email and if it were more than 5 sentences long, he would immediately close it and act as though it had never been received. Now did he tell anyone of this habit? No. Did he ever explain why he did this? Only if you were smart enough to ask. The only way you would even know to ask is to be in a meeting and understand that the questions he is asking indicate that he is not reading the information he is being sent!

He would never admit this is a group, but if you were to corner him in his office, during the 30 seconds that you might be allotted once a month, and you asked politely, he would tell you. What he would tell you was the same thing that you and everyone else in management already know, that is that you get X hundred emails everyday and that if your writers cant get the point across in 5 lines or less he doesn't have time to read it.

If you never had to work on a project with this man you were fine with your ignorance. Unfortunately the amount of vacation time I was going to be allotted one year was directly proportional to my ability to write a presentation FOR HIM that he would approve. Needless to say out of a potential 21 days of vacation, I got 4, however I also got the education of a **lifetime**. Contrary to what my wife's opinion of that year is, I couldn't afford to go to school and get the information that I learned from this one man in 14 days.

At the time I did not appreciate it, but what I learned is something that I have done my best to teach everyone who has ever asked me for assistance, and that is, if you can say it in 3 words why use 5? Remember earlier when I said join Toastmasters? Well that wasn't just a free ad for them. Toastmasters will teach you that when you have a presentation to give, it doesn't matter how *many* great stories you have, at 7 minutes and 30 seconds, they turn the lights off. What I didn't understand is that that equates to roughly 700 words (plus or minus considering humor and dramatic pauses).

Do not get married to your presentation material. Get married to your *message*, then delete everything else that doesn't apply. You will find yourself cutting out jokes, punch lines and everything else that YOU think is important. When you're primary thought is making sure that your reader / listener understanding your message, you will find that you are becoming such a better presenter, speaker and writer that you will not be able to comprehend the change!

4) **Decide EXACTLY what your team wants, and how that will fit into the over all plan.**

We may have covered this subject in greater detail elsewhere; however I would ask you to seriously go over a very important question: "Is there anything in life that I now KNOW that I wouldn't want to get involved in again?"

For example, although I had a great time and it lead to many great friends; the time that I spent working in the "fast food industry" was WAAY too long. At the time I needed a job with some steady income, and that's what it should have been, just a brief stop on the career train to help pay some bills. Instead, I found that I was having so much fun (I was the ONLY guy in a store full of women) that I stayed for over a year! Now admittedly, at the time I didn't think that I had much in the way of career options, but the truth was I just wasn't looking closely enough. Once I got tired of being broke I left there and went on in that same year to make almost $50,000 in the Photography business. Imagine what my life would have been like if I had stayed there 6 weeks instead of 16 months!

So when you look at your situation and what you want you will be gazing at concepts a little higher up the food chain that 'fast food', we hope. However, thinking this way **first** is going to prepare you for what's to come. Because once you look at your job on a very superficial level you will now need to look at it from a more specific angle. That angle is, the leadership position that you currently maintain, is it what you thought? Is it what was promised? Is it worth the compensation that you are generating? Now understand that we are not just talking about money here, but compensation in every form. I once went through a very heavy project and when working with a previous manager he would always find ways to "give" you time off to compensate for some of the over time that you generated. Well the new manager didn't quite think that way, as a matter of fact he thought it was all just "part of the job." Now for most folks that business as usual, but for one member of our team that was an insult that was NOT going to be tolerated. Although I would never question someone's health claims, it was very convenient that the week following our big project she suddenly developed a stomach illness, which required that she stay home, until a few hours after her daughter and grandchildren left town.

So I ask again, is your current situation providing you with adequate compensation for you to continue on in that spot for at least another year? If not, now is the time to let everyone know and to either straighten things out, or start looking for something else.

For example, at one of my large corporate spots, there was a **dramatic** difference in the amount of "availability" required between a team member and a manager. Additionally you were a specific type of high profile customer that the managers were required to not only deal with, but placate. One thing you must know when you move towards management is your limits, and you're other, more important requirements. I have lived as a millionaire and I have lived in places I wouldn't allow my wife to even know about. So I know that I can be very flexible in regards to my living conditions. My wife and child however, need never deal with such things. Therefore when the 'opportunity' for a move into management arose, I realized that I must be very specific about what teams I would and would not accept to manage.

I am more than confident enough in myself and my abilities to believe that I can manage *any* team, but at what cost? If I had to be on site or even on call 6 or 7 days a week, to make this team work like a team then I needed to wait and find another team to manage! What I told our Executive Level members of the staff was that there were certain teams for which I didn't feel that my knowledge or my management style would truly prove to be an asset. Therefore I would not be applying to any position to manage any team that I wasn't going to be able to enhance. Additionally, although this was for my information only, I would not find myself managing any team that was required to deal with any of the "high profile" customers that I had worked so hard to avoid.

The bottom line of course is, determine what is important to you, and how it plays in your life both in and out of the office. Many people are under the impression that throwing money at a problem will make it go away. My father always told me "Son, if money is your only problem you don't have any problems. You can always go make more money." When you combine that attitude with Thirty years of knowledge and experience of watching managers and owners try and solve all their issues through a thick application of green backs you notice something else. Money will smooth over an issue for a little while. Typically 9 to 12 weeks. After which time the person involved, even if it's you, gets used to the extra income and either starts to get restless, again. Or what ever it was that aggravated them in the first place comes back around and starts to bother them yet again.

Once you've applied a band aid made out of money, there is **no** amount that will ever work for very long. I once knew a manager who was very good at what he did. He felt a calling to attend seminary and leave a fairly well paying job. Well their well meaning and completely serious Senior Manager called them into the office and explained how valuable they were, by showing them what the salary would be if they stayed on and accepted "just a few more responsibilities." Well first of all I think you have **huge** cajones to think that you have a greater pull than God. But add to that the fact that you would actually want to hire someone who would say **no** to their creator, just for an increased pay check, and I just have to shake my head in amazement. Really, do you want an employee who said they felt a calling for ministry, but was willing to stay working for just "a few dollars more?" I wouldn't.

5) **Interview the person that YOU will be reporting to and make sure that your values are in line with his.**

Again, I believe that we have been through this fairly in depth in other areas, so I would suggest you look at them very carefully, but please pay special attention to the part about interviewing your boss. I have seen some folks get so twisted up with worry and anguish about just getting a job that they never even consider what working with the person across the table will be like.

For example, I spent a decade in Commercial Banking, at the time I was in a fast paced career building high energy, large income building mode. I had definite goals for my life and that included, making as much money as I could in as short a time as possible. I flew to Nashville to interview with the 3rd largest bank of its kind. I was so overwhelmed by the opportunity to meet my own goals with the income that was being offered, that I never took a moment to step back and look, or really examine the Administration of the company.

During my time with the President he kept telling me how great their compensation trips were, and they went to some of the best party spots on the planet, in order to celebrate their Top Achievers, an area I wanted to be involved with! The challenge was, I'm not a big drinker and never HAVE been. So when the boss kept coming back to all these alcohol fueled events it should have been a red flag.

To be honest, when the bank did what they were supposed to do, I made a lot of money for very little effort. The problem was, the administration was so wrapped up in their party lifestyle that they frequently let details slip through their fingers. Details like proper compensation, information, follow up and follow through. These were things that should be part of daily life in a bank that large. Believe it or not I actually dreaded their corporate "retreats" There were 4 of us who didn't drink and so in a group of 50 "professionals" there were 4 who stood out because we looked and acted like people you would want to entrust your business income to for growth and savings!

Please, take some questions into your interview with you, leave your judgments at the corner and make sure that you present yourself as "wanting to make sure that we are a great fit" rather than wanting to seek or avoid certain situations.

On the opposite side of the coin, if you are interviewing a prospective team member, and they ask you valid questions (how much is the pay, and can I have Saturday off, are not valid questions), about you, your team or how it all fits within the corporation you should be able to develop a few ideas about the person you speaking with.

First, they have probably read: Remote Control Professional (and if you haven't, shame on you!).

Next, they have done some research on your company or team and have some specific concerns or ideas that they want worked out, before they decide whether to accept a position on your team.

Finally, you are talking with someone who has done their homework. They have an idea on what it is you do, and either your description matches exactly or not at all, and they want to find out if what they see, and the way you manage are the same.

If, however you didn't interview your prospective boss on your way in, don't feel that it's too late. I wouldn't suggest this be attempted within your first six months, but if you forgot to interview your prospective boss and you want some questions answered, there is no time like the present. Again, just make sure that you questions are intelligent, well thought out, and relevant to what your manager does in his daily process. If you're just being nosy, believe me the manager will sense that and you have effectively shortened or stopped your forward momentum with that team, and you might want to look for somewhere else, anywhere else to transfer.

However, my experience has been that most managers who have been in their position any length of time will more than welcome you questions. Comments however, you probably ought to keep to yourself. Sometimes we get a little too comfortable with our superiors, even at their request, but it can come back and bite you very hard in the end.

6) Make sure you go in with the PROPER (positive) attitude, and decide what attitude you'll accept.

There are those folks who will always find something negative about any situation; you do not want to be one of those people. But just as important, unless you run a mortuary you do not want to hire these people. They are a dime a dozen and typically they will suck the life straight out of ANY project, even if the boss is the one who came up with it.

Conversely, if you come into the office or the interview whistling and happy even though the shock waves from Haiti have set Texas to rocking, that may be a little too much to the other end of the spectrum. Be positive, but find a happy median. If you're on the interviewer's side of the table, sharpen your people watching skills. Occasionally you will find people who really are happy all the time. Though they may get on peoples nerves every now and then, you shouldn't have to worry about whether they are following your instructions or not. Typically these are the northerners and they will do anything to stay on track for that gold ring.

Always remember, it's far easier to get folks to join you if your happy, positive and upbeat than if your full of doom and gloom. Dad always said that if you think your life is tough look around and you'll find someone whose life is even tougher. In 40+ years of applying that theory I have never had to look very far in order to fulfill that request. I won't bore you with the details, but I was born with a genetic issue that has made my life, physically, a little rougher than most, so I figure that if I have nothing to whine about than neither should anyone else. As a matter of fact in my entire life I have found 1 person who has it "bad enough" to deserve the ability to whine, and he was born without legs and 1 arm. So if he wasn't whining I figure I have nothing to complain about.

Now when you're the boss you get to set the attitude of the office, it should be positive, but we all have a bad day so eventually you're going to have one as well. How do you stop that from infecting you whole team? Well remember that 'muscle' we discussed? Part of your interview process for them is to make them understand that yes they are going to have a bad day, but they are NOT allowed to bring it into the office.

I once had a manager who told me that if I was having a bad day, then I needed to fix it, or stay home! I was the one person that everyone could look to when they were faced with a bad situation and I could bring them and their customer back around to our way of thinking. So if I came in and was having a bad day, that attitude had the opportunity to spread like wildfire, through the team and the customers. That's not a situation they could afford. So stay home.

Now if you're team's not in a position where you can have one or two folks off at any one time then maybe what you need to do is make sure that you can become the one person that they can always come to, why, because you cant afford to take time off. The challenge with you becoming that person is two fold. First off you then become "the guy" or "The gal", you really can never afford to take a day, evening or even an hour off if someone is working n your team. THIS will burn you out in a heartbeat.

The second challenge with you becoming the ONE is that it leaves you **zero** room for developing your ascension plan. Developing a plan of ascension is vital. I can not tell you how often I have seen people's careers put on hold while their bosses went looking for a replacement for them. Then when they decide to leave, suddenly opportunities start appearing! One girl in a very large corporation I was working with had a very specialized set of skills. No one wanted to learn what she did, so she was never able to train her replacement. Her manager was fat, dumb, and happy and so he never forced anyone to learn. Well she was getting paid so much money that the SR. Management finally started to take notice that fully 1/3 of this guys salary resource was being used on one person, so they told him she had to go. Not out, but elsewhere in the company. She was offered a job that fit her salary, she accepted it and then her manager started to search *nationally* for a replacement.

This poor young woman had her career put on hold for over **eighteen months** while they looked for someone else. In the end, She threatened to quit, and that's when they told her she could work part time, in both jobs (oh joy), IF she was willing to train someone. So she did, for six months she worked 2 careers while training one of the folks who didn't want to learn what she was doing all along!

Needless to say at the end of that time she was very worn out and I don't believe she will ever even hint at what she did before her current position. Now this wouldn't be a bad thing if it had actually spun off some way of making sure it didn't happen in the future, but the last time I knew that particular team still had no plans of ever developing a plan of ascension for anyone even their leadership.

Pain only hurts in two instances. First, while its actually happening. Next, if it continues to happen with no hope of relief coming!

7) Create the right image for yourself; PROTECT that image and your integrity that goes alongside it.

Far too often folks associate their "image" with those that Hollywood has created. If you're going to be a big screen movie actress, I guess that's probably not a bad idea. I mean if someone will pay you $20 million to stand and look good, your "physical" image can be whatever you choose it to be. If you're going to work in corporate America, your image is something that you should guard with your final breath.

I have spoken at length on dressing properly for the Job that you want, not the one you have, but your image and your integrity are two factors that can be changed in an instant, and it doesn't even have to be anything that you actually did! But be careful, those changes can be for the good OR the bad.

For example, did you know that in the Midwest recently a teacher of 10 years experience was terminated from her position because there was a video posted on YouTube of her partying? The bad part wasn't just that she was drunk and on the net. The bad part was that she let someone else take a photo of her and post it on the Internet, along with the date and time that it occurred. Her administrators happened to notice that this was the same date that she had called in sick.

Now I haven't seen this video, but I don't think that the picture was what got her fired, chances are pretty good it was the fact that there was proof of where she was and what she should be doing! Of course it could also be who else was in the video with her, and maybe a small part on what she was doing in the video. There's a story in the news recently of a "tweeny bopper" being caught by a cell phone camera smoking what "appears" to be a bong. Spin control of course claims it was "flavored tobacco" they just don't say what it was flavored with.

Now please, don't assume that I'm picking on poor old YouTube.com, the danger exists on almost ANY social Media site. Always remember though it doesn't even have to be a web site. There was a story when I was in school about a teacher who was terminated because she and an 18 year old High School Senior had their pictures taken in one of those $1 black and white photo booths. Apparently this particular 18 year old had a 16 year old girlfriend who found the pictures, got mad and mailed them to the principal.

Wait, the student was 18, what's the problem? Well the problem is that this teacher has crossed a line of "trust" with that student, her employer and most importantly the student's parents. As a parent I know my son is cute, but when I send him to school he better not be playing house with anyone more than 6 month older than he is! (By the way, my son is in Kindergarten, but you get the idea).

In another example, there was a small chain restaurant in the north that was just learning to use twitter to advertise their store. Sounds like a great idea right? Well during this experimental phase one of their managers sent out a 'tweet' with a coupon good for a "buy one get one" burrito coupon. Sounds like a pretty neat advertising ploy eh? Well he thought so to, especially when he started seeing customers coming in with the coupon. Feeling that he had earned his pay, he went home and went to bed. Unfortunately, when he sent OUT this coupon he didn't set any limitations on it. You know, typically a coupon will say "participating locations only" or "limit 1 per order", something like that. Well he didn't.

Now don't get me wrong, his coupon worked. It worked very well, and as a matter of fact it worked too well. Apparently there is or was a function in that sight that let's you send a tweet to everyone that is on your "following" list, thinking this was going to be magic, he used that function. The result was that although they "over" planned for a rush of 'up to' 1500 new patrons coming to their store, they instead found a line of over 9000 customers, all wanting their free burritos! Unfortunately the ingredients to fix a burrito are

very similar to the ingredients used in many of their other items. This resulted in them first running out of burritos then they started giving away Taco's, but since those were less than burritos they did a 2 for 1 on Taco's. Then they ran out of taco's and eventually moved down their menu until the store was completely devoid of ingredients by 2pm that day, and they had only served 4000 customers. Although they did offer coupons for a later date to the other 5000 customers, they were so angry after having waited in line (some for several hours) that the amount of BAD press that they received far outweighed any good press that they received.
Even a good idea can turn bad very quickly if not thought through.

Your integrity and your reputation are more important than almost anything else. These two things will be used as the yardstick to measure you against yourself in other people's eyes. Unfortunately in most cases, by the time YOU find out there is an issue with the way people perceive you, it's too late to do anything about it.

Last but not least, and this is for both sides of the table, watch who you are 'associated with' in your social web sights. Now this is not my personal opinion, it is merely corporate fact. More and more corporate recruiters are searching the social web sights to see who their potential applicants are spending their time with. I have seen more examples of this occur in public recently, and its getting more and more frequent.

I'm not a "Facebook/Twitter/Whatever" expert. But from what I can tell one of the greatest parts about social media is that they are like "classmates" was a few years ago. Along with everything else you can do, most social media sites seem to be areas where folks go to look up their old friends, and have fun with their current ones. Personally I think a resource like this is great. My mom's mom had over 47 Grandchildren and the majority of those have had children and some of them have had children. So that branch in my family tree is over 100 layers strong. Due to time and money constraints (and some desire) many of these folks I will never see again (granny died a few years back), however, through Facebook I know my sister has been able to keep in contact with "her generation" and their kids. So she has a connection to a great many of the branches that way. I think that's great.

However, on that same branch level there is a cousin, who had an 'accident' a while back. Lets say for examples sake that it was a hit and run accident involving alcohol and minors (it wasn't, but it fits the story). This accident has had a very detrimental effect on Cousin Ted, to the point where he started drinking more heavily and has been known to show up to the occasional wedding in cutoffs and flip flops. So let's say Ted has a Facebook page and he has connected with Sarah who is in his generation, and her page looks like it was created by an elementary school teacher who could give Mary Poppins a run for the money. Ted however decided to get a little creative on his. He decorated it with all these "Gothic" images and symbols, these dreary photos, and sound clips from "Death Metal bands." Lets say, on his 'wall' Ted goes on and on about these most graphic things that he would like to get involved with, if he ever were to run into "Today's" Disney Teen Queen. Then, just for fun, he goes to Sarah's page and says "hey check out My latest site."

Sarah understands where Ted is in his life, so she decides not to respond. Instead, however she had decided to apply as a Day Care worker at her local church. The church director, wanting to see what the world can see of Sarah, decides he will just punch her name into Google, and her Facebook page pops up as number one. He clicks on it, see's Ted's link and follows it through.

Now I wish it wasn't this way, but really what do you think the administrator is going to "see" when he connects Sarah and Ted together as family? He's going to see things that the press and parents would have a field day reviewing. Do you think I'm exaggerating? Recently there was an incredibly gruesome issue in a very small rural town north of where I live; the police reported to the media that "this kind of thing could have been prevented, if they had thought to look at the participants Facebook pages. Your mom always told you that you are who you hang around. Unfortunately in the digital domain this includes those folks that you know offline as well as the ones you know online, and the results can be just as serious.

8) Start early, work harder, stay later than ANYONE else, and watch for your teams to do the same!

This is another one of those items related to integrity and reputation; however this will only show once you are IN the office! Many folks believe that once they get past HR they are in for good, unfortunately that is just not true! I will admit that terminating an employee in America is somewhat harder than perhaps it should be, but almost any company worth its weight in salt will have a 90 day probation period where there is a zero tolerance policy in place. That means that any time within the first 3 months you can be let go for any reason, and they don't even have to tell you what it is, just let you go!

So while you are there, and you have everyone's attention (which you will) go ahead and establish a pattern for yourself. Make sure that your co workers understand that you are there to put in at least 40 hours of work each week. That means that idle chatter should be reserved for break or meal times. Knowing who won American Idol is not going to impress your boss. Him seeing you with your head down at your terminal 8 hours a day so that your prepared for 'the big meeting', will impress him. More to the point if your team knows that you're going to be in your office, working, not yukking it up with your leads, they are going to feel required to do the same. You've heard the saying "Monkey see, monkey do?" Well its just as true in a team you lead as it is in watching your 4 year old. To this day, I tell new employees that I'm here to do a job, if they wish to speak with me, save a seat at lunch. I teach everyone on my team the **golden**

rule on day one of their work experience. That rule is that if you listen to the rumors long enough, eventually they will become true, just about you! If you decide not to listen to rumors, and something bad is happening, trust me someone will come and tell you. You do not need to participate to get inaugurated!

Now, I am not saying that this is going to make you the most popular guy on the block, but you know what, you're not there to be popular. If you are a member of the team you have two jobs. First you are there to do whatever your administrators ask of you, assuming its legal ethical and moral. Secondly, and almost more importantly, you are there to make sure that you boss never gets surprised. You may think that knowledge is power, but let me correct you, the application of knowledge is power. People who are climbing the corporate ladder often confuse knowledge with application, so let's see if I can help you out here. As a team member, or even a member of management, knowing where the skeletons are buried is not nearly as important as knowing when to use that information.

We had a guy on a team once who thought that because he played basketball with the CEO's brother and got all this "insider information" through Sunday dinners that he should tell everyone what he knew, so as to raise the importance of himself in the eyes of the rest of the corporation. Unfortunately what happened was, everybody figured he was bragging (which he was) and thought he was just a jerk. Just before they lit the fires to burn him in effigy I pulled him into a closed door meeting and explained to him the theory of the value being in "knowing when to **use** your information", it did, unfortunately, take a few lessons, but he finally started to understand. Amazingly enough within a year he was awarded the first promotion he had been granted in over 5 years. This is someone who had over 20 years experience in this company and should have been very valuable to them. But because he couldn't figure out when to use the knowledge he had, no one else cared about anything else he knew.

If you are in the manager's chair you're reasons for paying close attention encompasses all those that are a 'team members' plus you have to watch out for the bottom line as well. You are there for one reason and one reason only. You are there to increase the bottom line incomes to your shareholders on every share of stock by wringing every ounce of productivity that you can from every member of your team!

Yes I know that sounds rather "rough" but it is 100% honest as well! I am not going to tell you that there is no "give" in the reason for you being there. I had a manager once who used to call my partner in her office every day and spent at least an hour every morning. Most folks in the office thought that he was getting the "inside scoop" on what was going on in the corporation. Well the truth was the Manger was an early bird, my partner was an early bird, so when they arrived in the morning, no one else was there, so they got to know each other pretty well. Then when the manager started having some issues at home and wanted to bounce ideas of someone else, they turned to the one person that they knew would be there, and could keep his mouth shut.

Now I tell that story for two reasons, first off, once the door is shut no one knows what's going on in there, and people will start to guess. As long as you and your employee don't come out of the office laughing it up, or worse, tucking in your shirts, your fine. The other is this manager is stepping over the same type of line that the school teacher was. That employee could have been a marital counselor on the weekends, and if so great, talk about it on the weekends. The employee also could have had some desires for this particular manager, and now the manager is making him think about things he ought not think about during work! (don't assume opposite gender in these stories, trust me it happens).

If you're careful and you follow some simple steps to guard your reputation and integrity two things are also going to happen, this time in your favor! The first is that you will earn the reputation as a hard worker. When it comes down to cutting the fat, last in first out is not always the way things move anymore. If you earn the reputation as a hard worker you are essentially making yourself irreplaceable! You will also find that you can do more in less time. Even if you don't feel that this is true, your supervisors will. Because compared to those folks around you who come in 1 minute before the timer goes off, clocks in and then goes to get breakfast, you will arrive a few minutes early, food in hand and ready to start working! In comparison you will appear to be doing more in less time, thus freeing you up for the really big projects that come across the bosses' desk!

9) ASK for what you want

OK, you are a hard worker, you get there early you stay late, you have made it through your first six months and your coaching plan, or yearly review is on the horizon. How can you make sure that when you leave the bosses' office you will be smiling? Simple, make sure that you very plainly and very simply lay out a set of plans that demonstrate why you deserve to be the salary that you are seeing.

Remember times are tough; everyone could use more money; however you are going to go into your quarterly review with a definite plan of exactly what it is that you have done for the company and how it could actually **cost** them money if you decided that you needed to go elsewhere. Write out a brief but detailed step by step outline of all the projects that you have been involved in, demonstrate the skill sets that only you have in your department and that even with that you can clean the occasional bathroom, if a raise were to make its way to you! No manager wants to spend money on training a new employee, but no company can plan on handing out raises just because its "that time of year again!"

Now, once you have this big plan and these huge detailed descriptions, how do you bring them up during your review/big meeting? You don't, you keep them to yourself until you're asked for them. Now before you start getting all tangled up in the details, understand that there are some very clever ways to make sure that those questions are guaranteed to be asked, and at exactly the right time.

Try this one on for size. You have been managing a new team for six months, your review is coming up because everyone gets their reviews at the same time every year instead of someone working for a year and then getting their yearly review. Makes sense, right? Yeah, I thought so to.

But that's company policy, what can you do about it? Well you can be as well prepared as you know how. So, this team you're in charge of has no history to be compared to, however each and every act of service is followed up with a satisfaction survey, of which we know only 5% are ever returned, and if they are multiple choice as opposed to fill in the blank the majority of the answers will be B (look I'm right).

As you should you have spent the week before your meeting gathering together reports, and customer service emails and charts, graphs and "supporting documentation" six ways from Sunday on each and everything you have done for the last six months? Included in all this documentation is any achievement, no matter how large or small, that any of your team has been awarded in that same time period. If somebody started in Toastmasters and won a contest, write about it, if someone volunteers for the homeless on the weekends, write it up. Everything that your team does, that contributes to the teams skill set, that the company is not paying for, write that down.

In relation to your team members, if they have assisted in the accomplishment of any event, or accomplishment of any other team, you want to **highlight** that! You also want to make sure to include a small file on yourself as well. However this file will be only about how you have helped, assisted or made possible members of your team get ahead in some way shape or form in life. If Bob bought his first house, make sure you document that even though he needed 3 days off for a moving closing date, you were able to jump in a perform his documentation duties, while he was out. Mary won an award as most improved bowler of the year award, make sure you document how much information and coaching you were able to offer, after hours, that helped her reach that goal, after all you cant talk bowling the whole time.

You're sitting across the desk from your Sr. Manager with a loose leaf book slightly smaller than a family size Bible, and you notice that there are less than 7 minutes left in your meeting and you haven't found anyway to go through any of this information that you have put together. What do you do? Well you take a slight chance, understand that this chance grows proportionally dependent on how many extra letters your Sr. Manager has after his name. PhD's MD's and M-O-U-S-E's hate to be interrupted, but if its something that will make them happy, they will tolerate it.

So as soon as he takes a breath you start with "John, I really think that we've spent enough time on me, and I know that I can only take up so much of your time, so if I may I'd like to show you some of the highlights that have occurred with the team this year..." One of two things will happen. First he will draw out his family's centuries old battle scimitar from merry olde England and separate your head from your shoulders. Or, and more likely, he will sit back and wait to be wowed by your team. You of course knowing that most Sr. Managers have the focus to last approximately the first 3 sentences of any presentation have "stacked the deck" with the best and the greatest team accomplishments that are not yours.

The reason why you wait until the last 10 minutes is very simple; he has his own form of the letter already mapped out in his mind. Your rambling on is not part of his plan, therefore taking the last few minutes will not require him to sacrifice too much of his plan in order to hear you ideas. Plus since your not technically talking about yourself, he will be a little more patient when listening to you.

So when do you get your time in the light? Well you don't, not where you can see it anyway. You make sure that your information is on the bottom, is brightly marked and possibly even printed on a different color or at least a different type of paper. As you wrap up your meeting you will present him with the folder of data on your teams highlights "in case he wants to get to know the individuals a little more thoroughly" and include yours as well. If I were a betting man I would give you very high odds that some how at the next managers meeting OR department meeting, your name and accomplishments are brought up. My CIO found out what my Doctoral Thesis was and thought it was so interesting he made it a point to bring it up along with how difficult it would be at least once a year in front of a department of about 4000 people,

Make yourself irreplaceable! Ask for what it is you want then demonstrate why it's worth it for them to award it to you.

10) Guard your integrity as though it were sacred

It is sacred, in many companies it is the only thing that you have that is generally recognized by the higher ups, so treat it this way. I know we touched on this previously, but it can not be stated emphatically enough. Your integrity will be "created" by what others see in you and then they will combine that with the way you treat everyone else around you, and come up with some composite picture of you that you hope shows your better side.

The number one way to generate a positive image of your integrity is to be truthful in everything that you say and everything that you do. You will find yourself in situations where being truthful could mean extra work or discipline of your team, and the choice is yours. Have your entire team mad at you for a little while, or have your bosses, never trust you with anything of any importance ever again.

This is what most people will see as a No win and in most folks eyes they see the statement "be truthful in everything that you say and do" as meaning, you need to be boring and inoffensive at all time. That is absolutely not what it means. As a matter of fact you will find, the longer you are in a position of leadership, the more opportunities there are for not telling 'quite everything 100% as it may have occurred.' I don't care who you see involved in that, and the longer you're in authority the more people you will see doing exactly that who will absolutely shock you, that is a habit you do not want to get involved. This is a habit that is very easy to start, typically it will be with 'the little things', you know fudging someone's time off, and lead to the huge things like, covering the real reason why the 'server upgrade failed' and took out 10 city blocks.

However, if your team knows that you're going to stand up for them, and stand behind the truth of a situation they are going to know exactly what it is that they should expect of you in ANY situation. Also they should understand what you expect of them in any situation. For example, we had a management change in a company in which I was working. The team had been managed by a former Army DI and he had created a habit for being truthful and for standing UP for everyone on his team! Now don't get me wrong, if you screwed it up, you paid the price, but the only one who was allowed to verbally abuse his team was him. There were numerous cases where one manager or another would run whining to Sr. Management about what an SOB this guy was, but typically when Sr. Management got to hear both sides of the story, what they found out was that they had tried to 'berate' someone on this mans team, without going through the manager first. That's just not the way you handle things if you're going to be a successful leader.

Far be it from me to try and tell you that you can't yell at someone unless they are on your team. But if you're smart you need to let that persons manager know what happened, and WHY you're going to do what you're about to do! Otherwise you may find a size 14 combat boot up, well, in an uncomfortable place, let's leave it at that!

Now when it came time for a new manager to be selected the Sr. management was in quite a jam. I had been very adamant about not wanting to mange that particular team, and they needed my manager in another spot ASAP. So they did the only thing that they thought prudent, they looked through the remaining members of the larger team and looked for someone that they thought could fit the role, and had been mentored enough by the previous manager to be able to step right in and run with it. When asked about their choice the previous manager thought "that's a great idea," after all it got HIM off the hook from managing 2 teams, and someone he had been working with got a boost up!

Unfortunately there were two major flaws in this plan, first the "mentoring" that had been going on between these two folks was strictly a one way relationship. You've seen those types of mentoring before, you do all the mentoring, the person who should be learning from you nods in agreement in all the right places but is listening to every 3rd word as long as it doesn't interfere with them updating Facebook. So although our DI was trying his best, in keeping with corporate culture, most companies still wont allow you to force your employees to 'drop and give you 20', just because they weren't listening, sigh. But his 'mentee' was listening just enough so as to not be reprimanded. The problem with this of course is that our manger was a real optimist, so when asked how the new guy would do he gave an emphatic "No problem, He'll be great!"

The second part was that the new manager had an issue that didn't get reveled until somewhere after the 90th day on the job. Well OK, he actually said the words "well if it can't be done between 7am and 5pm then I just don't need to do it. Now this is a very bad idea for an employee to have an attitude like this, I wouldn't hire it and I certainly wouldn't tolerate it on my team for very long. But when a manager is actually noted as saying those *same* words in front of another manager you know that this is something that is not a new idea, this is part of their makeup. It's the key part of someone's makeup that should signal many challenges down the road. This is certainly not an attitude that you want duplicated throughout your team or your organization! To make matters much worse, this particular manager actually stated this exact same idea in front of several members of his team one morning when he was asked about a particular task. Most of the managers seemed to be investing a great deal of overtime into this particular project. This is definitely not an attitude you would want to duplicate.

So, from what you've seen so far what points of integrity can you spot? First off, in the positive was my being very open with Sr. Management about what and why I would or would not lead a team. Next my former manager in being willing to drop what he was doing to help fill in an ailing team. The grey area comes in with his resounding recommendation to Sr. Management, of his replacement. Now, there's no telling whether he would have been just as good or bad without it, but maybe if he had been a little more honest with what he saw as far as the mentees attention during their coaching sessions a different decision would have been made. Finally of course is the absolutely awful attitude of the incoming manager. This is an idea that regardless if those are your feelings or maybe they are worse, you do not want your Sr. Management or your team to know about them. There will be plenty of opportunities where you are going to ask your team to walk face first into the fire. They need to know what kind of leader you are, before they are willing to make sacrifices themselves. If they know you won't go the extra mile, why would they?

11) Be FUTURE oriented in your life and your work

Famed Irish Statesman Edmund Burke once said "If we do not learn from history we are doomed to repeat it". I believe that this is a great place for a quote such as this to fall. We have all done things in the past that were not 100% successful. There is nothing wrong with that, as long as no one was hurt, learn your lesson and move on! Or, equally as important, if you perform flawlessly remember exactly what it was you did and how you prepared for the event, so that you may repeat it in the future.

Look ahead, 6 months and then again 5 years. Is that sufficient time to master what you want to master and allow you to move forward from there? Even if you don't believe that you will be where you want to be, you will be somewhere at that point in time. Can you determine where it is that you'll be, so that you can take events into account and utilize them to your own advantage? With proper planning and a future orientation, you will be.

Now is not the time for myopathy, create a long term vision and make sure you share it with the folks around you! Only in doing THAT will you be able to add their efforts to your own, so that you all get something new in motion. Find out what's next for your life. Most importantly share it with someone for whom you will feel accountable. When I sat down to publish this series, I wanted to make sure that this wasn't just "another one of those great ideas" that never gets followed through. So I carefully laid out my plan for my wife, including how she could play a major role. However I soon found a flaw in my theory. As much a it would pain me to have to explain to my wife, why the books hadn't gotten finished on time, but by assigning her such a major role I had taken away one of the most powerful tools to motivate myself. After all if I did my part and she didn't do hers, I could always blame her right? Wrong! When you look to the future and you set a goal, then divide the remaining time into manageable pieces, make sure that they are of a size so that if whomever you have assigned them to is not able to finish them on time (other people have lives too you know), that you have enough time to do them.

I learned that the hard way at work one day. I had a project due on a certain date, and to make sure that everyone felt included I sent appointments to one of my team members with the idea, that he's a big boy; he can look at the calendar and see when something is due and when he should start working on his part, right? Wrong! Therefore the day before the whole thing was due, when I casually asked "So your part will be ready tomorrow right?" His eyes got real big and he said; "Tomorrow? I thought they were due next Friday? Can you guess what I spent the entire rest of my day doing? Right his portion, and in my case I was able to perform it well enough that no one was the wiser.

However, in an effort to try and make sure that didn't happen again, I went to my manager when it was all over and explained what had happened. In all my years in business I had never experienced that because I only hired folks who were mature enough to take responsibility for their own results. This particular individual however had taken it upon himself to create his own time lines, which had nothing to do with reality. So I asked what I should do, my manager wisely related a similar instance he had had and explained what our Sr. Manager had done in that situation, and that is to set reminders on the calendar for regular 'progress checks.' Well personally I thought that was overdoing it just a bit, but hey what I was doing wasn't working so I needed to try something else. So the next time an opportunity came up I made the assignment and sent out check points.

You won't believe what I found. I found that I not only had to perform verbal checkups but visual checkups as well. In other words when we met he would 'tell' me how great things were going. But half way through when I asked to see his work, I discovered that what he was writing had zero to do with the project. Here I had asked what color a car was and I was getting the plans for the molecular composition of the rubber to be used in the tire! I know that this seems far fetched and your thinking that there is **no way** this guy could have been like this, but I knew I was in trouble the Monday he came to work talking about the dozens and dozens of hours of overtime he had worked the previous weekend (unapproved OT of course) and yet when I asked for a half way check point, he didn't have one!

If you think that your Sr. management is not looking down the road you are sadly mistaken, the distance "down" that road that they are looking is directly proportional to the seniority of their position, and that's the way it should be, until it gets to you!

You need to look as far down the road as your farthest forecasting level of management. You do this for two reasons, first so that you can see where the corporation is going, most importantly however is so that you can better prepare for what you're going to do when you get there!. The caveat of course is that your most senior management has a benefit in that they have been briefed sufficiently so that they have a very clear idea of where their going and what it takes to get there. You on the other hand, its going to get fuzzy the farther out you look.

Here's a good example. I was involved with a company at one point where a major change in command structure took place. Essentially the CEO retired (for the 2nd time in 10 years?). His replacement brought with her a LONG ranging 10 year plan. Now the outgoing CEO may have had a 10 year plan, but you would have never known it. For him as long as you made it through the year without going too far into the red, it was a good year.

So in comes a brand new CEO who had just attended this great "Future" seminar and brought all the ideas and vim and vigor back with her and laid out this grand 10 year plan. This was a great plan, very forward thinking and very progressive. She then spent 3 months going from department to department exposing everyone from VP's to Housekeeping to this great plan.

Much like the US Government, in none of these meetings did she ever talk about how to pay for all these plans. What do you believe was the one question on the minds of everyone in a "white collar" position? Right, "How are you going to pay for all this?"

What had happened was this new CEO went into a series of closed door conferences, accompanied only by her personal team of "yes men" and was exposed to a bunch of really great ideas that were being implemented by the "model" of their industry. That company was privately owned and had very expansive financial resources. Did I mention that she was CEO for a privately held **not for profit** company? No? OK, well for those of you who are not familiar with the phrase, "Not for Profit", accountants look in the bank at the end of the month and if there is money in it they say "Wow where did that come from?"

So she came back and based her entire career and the future of this entire corporation on decisions made in a vacuum. This is a bad idea, however she knew this was a bad idea because her predecessor had tried to do the same thing 2 years before, having press releases, parties etc, only to have to retract every single bit of it, less than six months later.

So, how do you prepare for your future when your CEO is making decisions in a vacuum, and you are in management, but at the level where it is your job to make sure that your team completes every task on time and under budget? Well you start staffing your team with people who can operate with very little supervision, and can report to you their progress on a regular basis.

With that as a team, you can know that every task you are given will be completed on time and without issue.

The opposite to that is you maintain your staff as it is, encourage them to learn more and more about what your company plans on doing, and trying harder and harder to not only understand it, but learn how to deal with it.

So you either staff up in preparation, or you sit back and watch it happen? Which one do YOU think is a better idea?

"The Best way to predict the future, is to CREATE your own future" – **Craig Mactavish**, Coach of the Edmonton Oilers

12) Be goal oriented in everything you do

If you get nothing else from this book, but the understanding of how important this idea is, you have recouped your investment. If you get up every day with your goal in mind, and ask yourself at each step along the way, will THIS help me get closer to my goal, then respond accordingly, several things will begin to happen.

First you will find that there are dozens of things that you do every day that have nothing at all to do with your end result. Some of these are simple, like getting to the coffee maker 1st at every fresh pot. Some of them are just down right unhealthy, being the first one at the box of donuts every Friday. But if you ask yourself at every point, "will this help me reach my goal?" You will find that there are certain things that you just don't need to be doing anymore.

Now, please, if you own stock in Dunkin Donuts don't get mad; let me give you an example of a pretty typical day for most folks in any office.

You're Goal: *Become the person that you're Sr. Manager Chooses to head up a new project:*

Believe it or not it can actually start the night before. Let's say you have to be at work by 0800, but like we talked about earlier you want to get there a little earlier, so you have decided that 0730 will be early enough to get a jump on your work, but not too early for your boss to be upset about overtime. Well in my house if you need to be somewhere 30 minutes earlier you need to get up an hour earlier. So instead of 0600, now you need to get up at 0500, why? Because maybe like me you just move slower than you used to when the sun isn't up yet!

So you're on the couch watching TV, typically you will watch the news then catch a monologue, and you start to realize that the distance from midnight to 5am is really much shorter than you thought. So, do you watch the rest of the game and the news, or do you go to bed at 10pm? If your goal truly is to get your manager's attention in a positive way, you need to turn the lights out and start sleeping by at least 11:00pm. This does not mean brushing your teeth and putting the kids to bed at 11:00pm, this means lights out, asleep! So your kids may not like it but if it's your job to put them to bed, guess what? Yes, they are going earlier too!

Monday morning rolls around, and like most of us, you reach for the snooze alarm, after all 5am is no time for a sane person to wake up is it? Unless you want to get to work earlier, at which point you need to force yourself out of bed and immediately into the shower. I'm finding that English Breakfast Tea can be a big help in this.

OK, you're dressed and on your way to the kitchen for that 1st cup of coffee, what do you do while you're waiting? Read the paper? Read a book? How about make a lunch?

Even if your company covers you for a 30-60 minute lunch break, you can save money and time by bringing it yourself. No you don't get to hang out with the guys and hear about their weekend parties while chewing a bad burrito, but you are also closer at hand in case the boss needs you.

Please understand, I am not an advocate of eating lunch at your desk, get out, run your toes through the grass, leave your office for a little while, but that doesn't mean you need to leave campus! I actually worked for a company once whose office was in such a bad part of town the pizza places would not deliver, but I always left my desk for lunch and found something to read!

So, you're on your way to work, if your typical it's between 30 – 45 minutes, what are you doing? Well again most folks are listening to the radio. But you're not like most folks are you? You have a goal, something that you're actively working towards. There have been studies that have shown that listening to audio programs about a subject that you wish to learn, for 1 year, are equivalent to a semester of college. So your drive to work is worth about $4500 dollars a year, in school tuition. What should you be listening to? Something that relates to your industry! Maybe your industry is So specialized that there are **no** programs available, great let's learn about people and how they relate (the number one requirement of most leads / managers / supervisors) so you start looking into Zig Ziglar, Brian Tracy, Tony Robbins, many of these audio programs can be borrowed for free from your library!

You get to work, you're earlier than most of your friends and you find that your moving a little faster as well, you finally have caught up to the fact that you are actively working towards your goal! You head for the coffee pot, there's no one standing there talking, but there's no coffee either. Throw some in the pot, head to your desk and log into your PC, by the time it boots up, your coffee is ready! You're back at your desk reviewing the day to come and the "usual crew" hasn't even started to trickle in yet!

Look at everything that you have accomplished and its not even lunch time yet!

Have we done anything revolutionary? Well if you consider reclaiming 2 hours of your day revolutionary then yes I guess we have, but in reality you have taken the first steps to starting your day the same way that the winners do! Which winners you ask? Pick an industry. Steve Jobs, Donald Trump, pick you industry and talk to your highest producers, I'll bet that their day is looking a lot like yours is, now!

Lunch is over, the "crew" is coming back, as they pass by your office, and you start to hear the comments about "how weird it is...", "I can't believe...", "You'd never catch me...", from the folks you used to talk with during lunch. Make a note of who says what, not a mean vindictive list, as a matter of fact its probably best if you don't write it down, just keep a mental tally. You're going to go over that list twice.

The first time will be at about 3pm that same day, start looking for the folks who were making those "I never" comments. Try and find them, I'll bet Colombo himself couldn't find them. Most of them have all started the afternoon slide. Some of them are sliding to the vending machines looking for that donut or cracker fix, to get them through the end of the day. Some of them will have started to slide towards the door, pulling excuses, usually about their kids, or parents if they're single. Just note who it is that's actually working after 3pm, everyone else is.

The next time you're going to go over that list is during the announcement of your next promotion. The folks that are genuinely happy for you, the ones who are really excited, will not be on that list. Now they may have been on the list the first day, but by the time your promotion comes in, some of your true friends will no longer be on your list. They will have seen the "light," they understand what it is that you're doing and how it is working, and some of them will have joined you!

The folks that are still on your list, and unfortunately it will be more than less, will be 'snarking', and sneering and complaining about how 'unfair it is' that they got passed up 'again.' You and I both know however that they did get passed up again, and again and again, that's how younger stronger, faster folks seem to accelerate in their jobs so well. The ones that are still on the list will be the folks that are just not finding the time for, because you realize what's working and what's not, what's making YOUR long term goal happen, and what's not.

13) Be RESULTS oriented in your actions

Wow, you really thought we would have covered this in the last section wouldn't you? Well OK, but lets get a little more specific and talk about you for a minute. Get out a clean sheet of paper, a pen that you know writes, turn off your phone and your PC and ask yourself the following "What can *I* and **only** I do, that if done well, will make a real difference?" Write that down, it may take one sentence it may take a page. But at least now you have a definite idea of where you're opportunity to plug in and add value.

Now when you're making this list you want to consider several different things, and keep them in mind as you're making the list. First you have already set your 'long term goals' so that they are in line with your Sr. managements goals and vision. Now you want to break down their long term plans into 1, 2, 5 and 10 year pieces (if management's vision is longer than 10 years out, don't worry about anything past that). Then look at the skills that you currently have and determine which skills you have that fit into that goal in that specific time frame and write it down.

Then take that same piece and flesh it out with each of the time segments along the long term vision and determine where your opportunities will appear to do two things. 1) Look to see where your skills will become unique 2) Next determines when they will require a "bump." Now the 'bump' is 2 fold. First you're bump in your skills. For example if you're in IT and you plan on being in your company for 10 years but have no plans on furthering your education, you will either not be there 10 years or you will be required to go to school. Next you need to see where your skills are so unique and so valuable to the plan that you deserve a 'bump' in your salary/position.

If you spend some time to do this properly you can practically lay out on the calendar exactly when, where and why you're promotions are coming. Consequently you will also be able to plot where along the time line that you need to be in class upgrading your skills!

Next and this is probably the biggest opportunity for you to grow, ask yourself, and answer, (preferably in writing as long as you have the pen out) what's the most valuable use of your time right now? "

In other words what actions do you feel have the most value, that only you can accomplish, given the time that you have. That "time" could be your current moment, this week this month, or this quarter." Lastly, and this is the big one, "Are you doing it?" If your answer is anything but a resounding **absolutely**, you have now isolated your most basic issue of your goal achievement. Like most of America, you have a great idea, and you're just not doing anything about it!

In the position of leadership you are going to find that one of your greatest challenges is in teaching this concept to your team. Unfortunately America has become a country where good is rewarded and adequate is now the goal. You probably know by now that I have a problem with this mindset. One of the biggest issues I have is that it has turned one of the greatest workforces in the world into a country where mediocrity is now the goal that everyone wants to strive to attain. When you create a team for your company and you are starting with folks who believe that average work is exceptional and that doing your assigned tasks should earn you something extra, then you have a very large problem on your hands. Unless you hire nothing but folks with north pointing compasses, you have a lot of work ahead of you.

Your best defense against creating a team of 'ordinary' comes during the interview. Now if, like me, you find yourself in a situation where you don't always get to pick your team members, and instead you are assigned folks from all over the company for various, non skill related reasons.. Realize one thing, right from the start; your folks probably do not fit well anywhere else in the corporation. I'm not trying to insinuate that you have an entire team of ": sweathogs" (now that's showing my age), but that they probably did not fit in the team or with the manager that they came from.

Here's a perfect example. I was given a team and an entire department, and told that in the next 6 months I needed to stream line the team and the processes, or I needed to consider clearing the team and starting over. Taking this as a challenge I looked at exactly what the team was being asked to do. I then took it apart one process at a time. In doing so I uncovered a huge waste of duplicated efforts. So I told my superiors, that either these team members needed to go, or I needed more work to give them.

"But," they said. "We've been told many times that, that team is at 100% capacity." This was a true statement, once you figured in all the coffee runs the Internet surfing and other non corporate tasks that were being done every day, all day on the clock. So when I asked for more work, they gave me another application to watch over and told me that if the numbers started to slip it would reflect poorly on me. One month later I was back again asking for another application. Six months later this team, was cut by 50% (the other half having transferred to their teams) and had grown from 1 task to 8 applications. Add to that we were the most efficient, effective team in the department and had the highest customer approval rating of any team, and you can see, that by being proactive and expecting more, I was able to get MORE done with fewer hands. Therefore by keeping my focus, and thus my team's focus, on our outcome, I was easily able to surpass all expectations.

14) Be idea Oriented in your work

This may seem like a restatement of what we have already talked about, but remember if you are not willing to "put yourself out there" you will *never* get any results that you need.

Whatever it is that you do for work, whether it's as an auto mechanic, administrative assistant or Cloud Computing Programmer, as you do your work, ask yourself in what ways can some of your processes be made more efficient? Is there a better, faster or less expensive way for guests to your company to find out where "Bob Stevens" is, than go to the administrative assistant and query them?

I worked with a company once that had corporate campuses spread out over 3 counties. There were people coming and going on these campuses like they had never heard of security. Well one day apparently someone scared an administrative assistant of someone who made 6 figures so they decided to implement some security. To make this one employee feel better, they decided they would start in that building.

Being a large corporation they did what most big companies would do in that situation, they looked for an automated unattended way of making this building more secure. This succeeded in locking an entire floor of employees on their particular floor; they could neither enter nor leave.

Not being satisfied with that solution, they moved their security net so that it would encompass a larger area, thus providing more security, and requiring even more technology. This resulted in locking an entire building out on the streets. This time the people inside could go home, they just couldn't get back in the next day.

Next they decided to hire a real live human to sit in the lobby every day, all day and ask folks to sign in, and "by the way, who are you looking for today?" When they first placed a person in that chair, they built a whole desk and checkout system around them, and the team member was an older employee who no longer qualified for the job they had, but they couldn't terminate. That is not the best face you want greeting strangers who are already mad because they are lost! So then they moved to a college student who was very pert and very pretty and very smart. This was a great idea, she was a huge help to customer, clients and employees. At least she must have been, otherwise why were there always such a huge group of young men gathered around her desk morning, noon and night?

Finally they hired a very nice person whose primary qualification was that she wanted to be there in that kind of a job! This job does not require a degree; it requires few specific qualifications other than the ability to find your way to work. However 9 hours a day, 5 days a week, you had to be in the same spot, rain or shine (this was a well air conditioned area with lots of glass), have a smile on your face and be able to gently guide people where they needed to go!

Are you seeing the situation here? In trying to solve a rather simple problem they spent many thousands of dollars as well as job opportunities for three people, and opened up an entire team of young men to the "grey area" of emotional indiscretion.

Remember, although this idea requires you to be creative you also want to be cost conscience. Just like you may find it harder and harder to make it between paydays now days, your company may not have an unlimited supply of cash either!

No matter how good an idea is, no matter how much time or energy and idea can save, the bottom line is, is it feasible? Also ask yourself if it's a change to change or is it actually needed?

One company I worked for has employee parking (including handicapped parking) 6 blocks away from the building in which the majority of the folks parking there, worked in every day. Needless to say in inclement weather, this solution rapidly showed many of its flaws. So the company hired 6 full time employees and purchased 3 large "mini buses" in order to shuttle the employees back and forth. Interestingly enough, none of these "shuttles" had handicap access. For several years many people everyday, including those who could very well have needed the exercise, used these shuttle facilities. Then during a quarterly review it was noticed how much these 6 salaries and 3 buses were costing, so the company terminated 6 people, and parked the 3 buses. Then come storm season it was determined that "during inclement weather" there would be some assistance provided.

I'm not sure where you live, but at the time I lived in a pretty nice (climate wise) area, so I assumed as soon as rainy season stopped, so would the shuttles. No, instead they got more complaints from folks riding the shuttles that they were running late every day, because the shuttles were not running on time, or there weren't enough of them. Then the corporation instituted a new rule that stated that anyone driving a company vehicle, who saw someone waiting for, or needing a ride, for any reason, was required to stop and give them a ride. Thus assuring that at least 20 separate occasions each and every day, employees (most of who worked on an hourly basis would stop and pick up "hitch hikers."

Help me out, in the midst of one of the worst economies since the depression, the company lays off 6 folks and replaces them with 20 "part timers." Are you following my problem here? So yes, be idea oriented, but do your best to think that idea as far through to the conclusion as you possibly can! Only in this way can you stop yourself from performing such inane procedures as the ones you may see here.

15) Be PEOPLE oriented in your activities

When I first started working with computers there was a movement towards certifications. Everyone needed to be "certified" in one form or fashion to make sure that they were the on the cutting edge of knowledge. Each of these certifications of course, came with its required schooling, which came with its required fee. In the end two things became very apparent; first the folks providing the certifications were also tied into the education, meaning that they were profiting several times by promoting the concept of certification. But more importantly came the concept that there was a very definite ceiling associated with "playing with hardware." The real money, and the risk, was in working with people, not things. Therefore I had to start learning how to work with people, both alongside them as peer's and more importantly, in teams where I was designated as a lead, most opportunities like that came merely from volunteering.

Once you find yourself in a position of leadership, be it a team of 2 or 20, and make sure you lay out a VERY clear idea of exactly what it is that you are prepared to do for your team members! If your organization allows it, you take the target, let them take the glory. Credit should *always* follow its own path back to good leadership. However anytime I have found myself or anyone in a position where they are trying to make themselves look good at the expense of others, they inadvertently alienate their team, and make themselves look much worse before they started. Being in charge is not about walking softly, sitting behind a desk and carrying a big stick. It is however about getting into the dirt besides your folks, leading from the front, not directing from the rear! Additionally keep in mind that credit goes to your team and problems stay with you. That's where they land anyway! By accepting responsibility for the bad and giving credit for the good you are giving your team the chance to say dozens of great things about you as a leader.

Next, talk with *your* leaders and find out from them what it is that they want you to achieve with "their" teams. They are the one's ultimately responsible to the corporation. Then as you start to approach that goal you will find out that you are given more opportunities to meet with them and receive slight course corrections for the tasks that you have. You will then want to meet with your teams and offer them the slight corrections they may need. Is this a good thing? Absolutely, after all how often is a plane directly on track to its destination? Well if you follow FAA statistics, only about 9% of the time. That means that over 91% of the time they are either off course or correcting from being off course. Let your leaders know what you want to accomplish and then make sure you follow up and follow through by spending some time checking in with them and letting them know how things are progressing. From where they stand they may have a view of a much different picture than you do, so they can guide you and keep you on track! But most of all this will allow your superiors to actually see tangible results of the value that you are creating for them.

Finally, remember that money will only resolve a person's problem for a very short period of time. Often an employee or team member will come to you with an issue, sometimes even a very personal and private issue, and look for a solution. We as leaders are being called upon in these situations to stand up and take control of our teams. We are not being asked to 'sweep it under the rug' or defer the question somewhere else, especially if your team knows you have resolved these issues in the past for someone else! In the case where a team member comes to you and tells you that "something has come up" and they have an opportunity to move elsewhere, whether its across country or across town, regardless of the reason that they are telling you, very rarely is money the real issue.

I can't tell you how often I have seen an employee go to their Manager or Director or superior and tell them that they must leave the team because they have been offered **X** job with less stress and more money, only to have this intelligent and capable director try and counter with more money. If you do that you are focusing on the wrong part of the conversation. When John comes to you and says that ABC Company has offered him to do the same job for 10% more money and no on call, the 10% increase is not what you need to pay attention to, it's the **on call**. Now I'll be honest with you, in most cases, by the time that team member has screwed up the courage to come and give you the appropriate lead time for their leaving, they have already set in their mind exactly what their new working environment will be like. When that has happened you actually no longer want that employee, they won't be doing a good job for you. Even if, through some miracle you offer them 12% and they determine to stay, I can promise you a few things. First, you will *never* get the quality or level of production that you once did, from that employee. Next, they will remain, and be content only until the 10% no longer makes any difference in their lives. For example if John wants his wife to be able to stay home and raise his boys, but because he doesn't earn enough with your company he must send his wife to work part time, you could offer him a raise equivalent to his wife's years salary, and he will stay. But he will only stay until he gets accustomed to having his wife home, and ABC Company offers him 10% more than you're paying him now! Then what can you do?

16) Be Growth Oriented

By now you must be starting to see a trend. Many of these concepts are starting to look and feel related? Congratulations you are on your way to the top. When things start to come together and you can see the common threads and how they all start to work together that's when you can finally say to yourself that you are well on your way to where you want to be! I had a Professor in college once that called it 'mental maturity'; in that case it wasn't so much about solving the problem as understanding the path that you would take to solve the problem. Once you understood that you could solve almost anything.

However in order to truly become growth oriented you will find that developing a love for life long learning is a must! There was a young woman who came to me with tears in her eyes, just begging me to spend some time with her so that she could learn to do what we do. As you progress you will find that people will do one of two things, either they will tease you for wanting to excel or they will look for the 'easy' way to achieve what you have. Remember when folks give you a hard time for wanting to excel in life, that's just them trying to justify to themselves why they aren't going anywhere.

So here was this young lady just begging me to help her, so I did what I have always done in those situations, I lay out for her exactly how it was that I started down this path. I wrote out the titles and authors of about 20 books that I feel need to be read in order to truly get a handle on where you want to be in life. Her response would have disappointed me, had I not heard it dozens of times before. "Yeah, I know all about that, but what about the rest of it." So I carefully explained that the "books will help you build the foundation you need to start on this journey." She then explained to me that she didn't want a journey, just a result.

So, if that's what you're looking for, I can assure you, that you will definitely find many tools here that will start you on the course of where ever it is that you want to be. But that's all it is, a beginning. If you want something that will work for you for the rest of your life, you will need to commit to **learning** things for the rest of your life!

Why is that? Two reasons really, in most technical areas of expertise, knowledge has a half life of about 2 ½ years, which means that what you learn on your job today, will be of almost **no** use in 5 years. Now, this is not to say that the core of what you do will be of no use. But the details will have changed so much that you will either spend the time to learn what you need to in order stay current, or find yourself in need of a new job!

I know what you're thinking, "OK Smarty pants, and how can I stay current?" It's actually very simple, and some of it we have touched on before. First make sure you read at least one hour a day, *in your field*, every single day! Now unless you are in certain adult oriented entertainment industries, reading romance novels does not count! However, you would be amazed at what would fall into that category. Work for a bank? Read some of the autobiographies of the great financiers of the last 200 years. Donald Trump, Ross Perot, Warren Buffet. Are you in management? Wow the choices are almost mind boggling, but for a good start look at some of the classics; Napoleon Hill, Og Mandino, Zig Ziglar. Are you an Auto Mechanic? How about Henry Ford, John Delorean or Lee Iacocca? No matter what your field of interest is there are volumes written on how to do what you do, better. But almost as important as discovering how to do your job better, you will discover the mistakes that people made while building their businesses. Typically most biographers will explain the mistake, explain the solution and then give you a step by step walk through of exactly how that solution was executed.

Next is something we did cover in an earlier section, and that is to turn your car into a rolling university. Most workers spend between 500 and 1000 hours a year in their cars! If you converted that time into an audio library that would be the equivalent of 2 full time college semesters every year! Again, regardless of what your industry is there are seminars and courses being offered all over the country if not the world, that you can find on recorded media to listen to while you commute. This of course lends itself to the idea that if you can actually attend these seminars and courses you can not only obtain the information first hand, but get the recorded version to re-enforce the information once you get home!

Many folks believe this may be overkill, but anytime I attend a seminar or learning class, I take notes throughout the entire time. A very wealthy man once said that sometimes you won't be writing down what the speaker said, but what you thought of, when he said what he said. He stated that this would be where you get your best ideas from! Therefore I come back and take my written notes and then TYPE them up and keep them in a file on my PC. Not only did I hear it once, but that got re-enforced by me writing it down, which was then strengthened by my typing up my notes, which was much clearer when I was able to listen to the audio portion! Overkill, maybe, but you can never say I wasn't familiar with the material.

Not to beat the obvious into the ground, but I will share this with you. I was at work and there was a great deal of noise going on around me, it had been my habit to simply play some music on my PC, but that day I had stuffed a bunch of DVD's that I wanted to watch into my briefcase. Forgetting that my PC had a DVD player, I pulled out my headset and was going to plug in one side when I came across the DVD's. Now I am not suggesting you watch movies at work! But what I found was that by using Windows Media Player to play the DVD, and keeping my head set plugged in, I could minimize the "video" and still hear everything that was being said. Now since these were educational DVD's its not like I wanted to 'watch the movie' anyway, I just didn't want to give anyone the impression that, that's what I was doing. From that 45 minute 'video' I got the seed of an idea, which over the next several months I was able to develop into a full blown business plan!

17) Become EXCELLENCE oriented.

This one seems almost self explanatory, but for those of you who just picked up the book, flipped it open and landed here, let me elaborate. If you talk to anyone from the "Greatest Generation" they will talk very openly and frankly about the quality issues with America today. Now I don't just mean certain superstores whose founder would publicly state that to buy from his store was to buy American, even as he was mowing down mom and pop retailers like a tractor on a golf course. I'm not even talking about the fact that for 20 years "American automobile" was synonymous with over priced items purchased to send your mechanic's kids to college. I'm talking about everything else. I'm asking, why is it that every time my family drives through a certain "clown based" restaurant with big golden semi circles we get to play "bag, bag, guess what's in the bag" I'm looking at the idea that we say "thank you" to the kid who takes our money from us at the gas station even though he acts like we are interrupting his concentration on the cure for cancer. Yes, as an end result I am talking about the fact that there are SO few items that are stamped with **made in America**.

You have the knowledge, you have the training, and you have everything you need to become the best at whatever it is that you decide to do! Now it's up to you to actually put that all to use and become the best at what you do. The most wasteful thing in the world is unused information. Well, O.K. that's not 100% accurate. In all honesty the most wasteful thing in this world is untapped talent. It's watching the guy who retired from RCA with 75 patents in his name teach high school physics to a bunch of kids who only took the class because it looks good on their transcript. It's the woman who figured out how to feed and clothe 7 children while her husband was fighting on some other continent, and yet never asked for a hand out, is rocking her remaining years away to the Oprah Winfrey show. It's the most talented new managers in any companies' history being required to attend meetings 7 to 9 hours every work day, because Senior Management can't figure out a way to put a stop to all that nonsense.

In the end, no one really cares how fast you get your job done, if you then must spend an additional 50% of your time making it right! There was a Health Care organization once who signed a contract with a vendor for a product that didn't exist yet, however their contract required them to install and implement the program that the vendor did have, within certain time frames or lose out on millions of dollars in "rebates" (which is a whole other issue). So they pushed and beat and worked triple overtime in order to put in place a product that did not meet their needs or their expectations, just so that they could hit certain deadlines and receive a large percentage of their investment back from the vendor. Confused? Yeah I was to. It seemed to me that if you Paid $100 for a product, that came with a stipulation that as long as you installed it within 30 days you would get $90 back, BUT you had to pay $300 in over time pay, and then another $100 in fees for the product that you actually wanted in the first place, that someone's math just wasn't working out very well.

To compound that error, that company not only spent those kinds of dollars times 10's of thousands, but they missed their deadlines by over a year. Are you seeing where this is heading? Because they missed their deadlines for installing a product that they never wanted they lost out on the 'rebates' that were earmarked to pay for the version of the product that they did want, when, and if, it finally became available.

Some things you can not take a short cut to, quality being one of the big ones! The other side of the quality coin of course is integrity, but I have a strong feeling we have covered that one sufficiently.

How much extra time does it take to inventory a package before it is sent to shipping and then once more before it is sealed BY shipping, in order to avoid having to pay return shipping and probably a hefty discount on future orders to appease a customer who received the wrong item at the right time? It's still not the right product or the right time, because now it's later yet! But hey, remember you saved two peoples salaries by not having to hire the staff required to verify that what was in the box, matched what the customer ordered. If you ever find yourself in any project and you are being told, by a vendor, that everything will work great because of the new barcode scanning system, remind that vendor that the US Grocers Association has stated year after year that those scanners are incorrect between 30 and 35% of the time.

How much additional effort, does it take you, as a manager, to look over your employees before their first customer contact each day and make sure that shoes are tied, pants are buttoned and their **hair is combed**! Now the question of whether you should have to check these things is another matter entirely. You can know how to build a HD TV, but if I can't stand to be in the same room with you, I'm never going to give you a chance to show me how much you know.

Please, understand that I am in no way suggesting that as a manager part of your duty everyday is to make that every team member brushes their teeth and washes behind their ears. What I am saying is that as a manager it IS your responsibility to look at your team and know where your weak spots are, and if need be, pay a little extra attention to the folks that are in those jobs. Alternatively, if you can find a way to make sure that only your best and brightest are in those first contact roles, do so. Just prepare yourself for a larger amount of turn over. The best way that your employees are going to be noticed and therefore recruited right off your team, is to spend quality face time with those customers day in and day out. Those leaders who do that, and make an equitable use of the time will indeed find that they are gathering the positive attention of their superiors, and yours!

Become excellence oriented. It takes minutes on the front end for years of payoffs in the end.

18) Be CUSTOMER oriented in your business

Now I will admit, this one does tie directly in with 17. It can actually be seen as a natural extension, but watch closely, it makes a huge difference. Once again, what you decide to do for your work has no bearing on this section; no matter what you do you will have customers. Are you a computer programmer for the city water works? Your customers are everyone that lives in your area, combined with everyone else that works for the city water works. What you do affects every single one of those people. Treat them like they have control of your paycheck, because the do!

The statement "You must create and keep customers" will find root in every business. If, at this point, you know what your business is (look under elevator speech) then you can take that idea and determine exactly who it is that will best be served by your business. Once you know that, you now have a handle on exactly what the makeup of your audience is, and you can determine how to help them the most. The bottom line is exactly that, who are you helping the most and how can you best serve them.

Let's talk to Grandpa again, ask him what happened when he went to the appliance store to buy his first refrigerator after he got married. Chances are he will explain that he and the Mrs. saved for months if not years, before they decided to invest in a refrigerator. Then he went downtown to the appliance store where he was greeted either by the owner, the owner's son, or someone else that the owner trained and trusted with his lively hood.

That person, lets say his son, would greet you at the door, he was clean and nicely dressed, maybe not a tie, depending on whether they could afford an independent repairman or they still did the work themselves. The son would then spend a few minutes asking you a series of questions (no more than 7) that would allow him to lead you to exactly the unit that you needed, for your house and your financial situation.

Compare that with the last time you bought a TV. Chances are you spent 10 minutes wandering around the AV "department" of a superstore, looking for the origin of the Swedish speed metal being played at 11 on the loudest speakers available, so that you could think without wanting to hurt yourself. Once you found anyone wearing something that looked like the stores color scheme (typically they will be hiding under the largest item in the area), and gain their attention (remember Attention Deficit Disorder, that's a recent thing, Gramps doesn't have any idea what it means), you then wave several large bills in front of his face along with the pages of print outs that you brought from your HOURS of research on the internet, only to find that IF the TV you want is actually IN stock, it cant be delivered until the 4th Tuesday of the last month with 2 Full moons that ends in a Z.

If you do not relate to this story you either haven't bought a TV since Nixon was in office, or you're not paying attention. I actually buy many items online just so I am not *forced* to deal with the people who seem to have won the DNA lottery by surviving with less than a full cerebellum! The sad part of this whole scenario is that these people actually have the gall to call themselves "Team Members" or "Appliance Partners" or my favorite, "Audiotronic Specialists." All of these fancy words so that they do not have to be called salesman, after all that has such a 'demeaning' sound doesn't it? Absolutely not! If these folks had even one ounce of ability or knowledge they would be wishing that they had enough talent to actually be considered a salesman. As my dad always said, "Nothing happens until someone sells something."

How hard would it be for the Store Manager to clean up the area of his store that regularly brings in 10's of thousands of dollars every month? Not long, unfortunately he would have to go through the entire hiring and training process all over again, in order to find someone with fewer pieces of metal sticking out of their face than are actually in the manufacturing of the television! Worse yet, in order to get people to show up to work on time and well groomed you have to find what used to be called "nerds;" the problem with trying to hire these folks is that they have a business of their own selling or developing something on the web, and probably have a higher income than the manager does.

Also understand that if you happen to be dealing with someone who has a little grey around their temples, or is a business owner themselves, they probably have a little bit of that thing called integrity. I'm reminding you of this because one of the fastest ways to find yourself out of a sale is by 'bad mouthing' the competition. If the only good things I can say about my product is that it does things so much better than the other guy's, that should make you very curious about what the other guy is selling. That's the last thing I want. If I had been embellishing my products abilities at all or, making the competitions product sound so much worse than it actually is, you will never get a sale from most folks over the age of 40. Integrity is that important!

One last item to keep in mind for being customer oriented. Regardless of your business, when your customer is in front of you and he is comparing your company with another one and the only thing that you can come up with to differentiate yourself from the rest is cost, you *will not* make the sale!

Part of your customer orientation must involve finding out what is actually important to the customer, price will often play a part in making the decision. But if it is the only thing that you can demonstrate to your customer that makes your company different I can promise you 2 things:

1) If you are somehow able to make the sale your profit will be lower than you want it to be.

2) The loyalty of that customer to your store will last only as long as someone else doesn't offer them a better price.

The first thing is almost self explanatory, but in case you're still unsure, ask yourself this: How is it that your company is able to have a lower cost than anyone else? Either they are making a product with inferior materials, or it's coming out of your paycheck.

The second item again comes to rest right at your doorstep. Just because you have the lowest price this time doesn't mean that that you will always be able to beat your competition.

So with those things in mind, finding out exactly what is important to the customer now becomes a priority. Simply, it's all about conversation.

Let's go back to the big Electronics superstore:

You: So, Mr. Hess you're looking to buy a new TV, were you looking for LCD or Plasma?

Customer: What's the difference?

You: Well sir it really all depends on what is most important for your viewing, will this be going in your bedroom for you and the MRS. Or out in the living room for 5 – 6 people?

Customer: Well probably the living room, why does it matter?

You – It could very well matter a great deal on a package system, but for a larger group the viewing angle on one is much better than the other.

Customer – So it's different when me and the Mrs. are watching CSI than when me and the boys watch NFL.

You: Oh absolutely, do you often entertain for large groups in your TV room?

Customer: Well not too often, but I do need to make sure that we have a good picture during the season.

You: Well of course you do, and with that in mind a wall mount may not be as advantageous as a stand mount. Do you have any Kids at home?

Customer: Why yes, we had a baby about a year ago and….

Ok, now you know several things, first, he has an infant, so whatever you sell him you do not want on a flimsy table top stand you want a solid wall mount. Second, he does entertain occasionally, so viewing from wide angles isn't always a premium, so directing him towards something that has a narrower viewing angle might not be such a bad thing….

Wow, we learned all that just by keeping his needs in mind and not our paycheck.

19) Be Profit oriented

Ok, this one I have to admit, I am almost embarrassed to have to include. Then I have a meeting like I did the other night. A business owner was struggling to stay in business; he had been working "at it" for 3 years and just had not made that last big step towards being profitable. So I asked him to tell me about the last meeting that he had with one of his prospective customers. For the next 30 minutes he described in intimate detail a meeting in a business owner's office and how he had done everything that he could to make his business something that the other owner needed to be part of, and how well the two companies would fit together.

He studied the individuals business goals, let the customer talk far more than he did, asked what seemed to be the right questions, and then when it was all over, he left without a contract in hand.

So I said to him; "Jeff, it sounds like everything was going perfect. You had him interested you showed him the value of what you do; he admitted that even he could see a strong relationship with your company, yet you left without the contract. Why do you think that is?"

His response was typical, but" Well, Jerome if I knew *that* I wouldn't have to ask you!"

So I admitted that was a fair statement and then I asked him about his profit orientation, you can learn a GREAT deal about people by learning about their relationship to money. He, like most of us said he loved money, but of course, that's not why he did what he did…

Ok, I think we have started to zero in on our issue.

You appreciate what money can do for you, you are in a business that has the potential to make a lot of money, just by helping someone else get what they want, but "that's not why you do what you do?" I was clearly a very confused person at this point.

So I asked him, Ok, why do you do what you do?

His response started typically and spiraled right toward the heart of the issue "Well I love what we do, I know that we are saving our customers a great deal of money, and there is no better feeling than being able to use your skills to help someone else achieve their goals." Bingo!

"Jeff, which situation sounds better to you, helping someone achieve their goals, or getting paid to help someone achieve their goals."

See it seems as though he sat with a business owner for almost a half an hour and yet he never once asked for the money! "Oh, but J I *never* discuss money on the first appointment"

Wait you mean to say that you have the customer eating out of your hand, dying to learn what you know, and wanting to get your help with his business and yet you are going to make him wait a week before he can buy from you?

How many **second** appointments do you get?

"Well see J that's the hard part, getting that second appointment!"

Lesson learned, ask for the money, contract, deal whatever it is that you do, the only place anyone gets out from in front of me with out a signed contract is if we happen to meet in church, and even then I book the follow up right then and there. Now I understand that this seems like it would apply almost exclusively to sales orientated situations, but that's not true at all. If you are in a meeting with your team lead and you need him to assume control of a project that is foundering in its present state, how do you close your meeting? Because most of the meetings that I have been involved in, from the leads side, have ended without anyone confirming what the next step was, when it would be started, when it would be finished and what the checkpoints were along the way! Now I can hear all the folks screaming about micro management, but that's not the point at all.

Next time you have to turn something over to your lead, especially if it is something that someone else started, your parting comment could be something along the lines of, "I'm seeing this project as something that should take no more than six month to complete, how about you?" You have just set an expectation of successful resolution and put a time frame on it. Now your lead has the opportunity to either accept or reject your estimate, based upon their experience and teammates abilities.

I was asked once; if I thought that I would need any extra bodies the following year. Of course my manager, being brand new in his job, asked this as a casual almost back handed after thought. But since it was something that I had been waiting for I was prepared with this reply, "Well Bob, as you know we have just assumed control of the XYZ system, and it is taking up more of our time than we initially were budgeted with. When you factor in the fact that project ABC as well as application DEF and team QRP will all be experiencing updates over the next 12 months, I would suggest that as long as none of these items deviate from their projections by more than 10% we should be fine just the way we are. However, if we start to see more slippage in the DEF or XYZ stats requiring more than 15% of our resources we will definitely need at least one extra body. I know in the past some managers have budgeted in for a contractor for a percentage of the year. Thus granting a "temp" for part of the year, that way if things start to shift we could pull in some contract workers for the rest of the year an finish the projects next year with a clearer understanding of what we are dealing with."

See, I had not only given him an expectation of the positive, but also a quick overview of a worst case scenario. Additionally I had presented him a way to dig himself out of a potential hole, and done it in a manner that helped him save face. For this particular manager maintaining dignity was very important. Probably the only thing I could have added were regularly scheduled updates, but since he was new, I wanted to give him the chance to come up with *something*!

In referencing our original issue however, what you will find is that while you're waiting for your second appointment you are giving your customer time to think about every excuse in the world on why not to do business with you, and true to form they do exactly that. They take your ideas and either implements them in house, and fail, thus proving that not investing in you was a great savings. Or they go with the option that cost less than yours, once again failing, but it was probably being blamed on you again anyway.

Or worse, they tell the next guy who sits in their office what he learned from you, and that guy says "Oh boy we can do all that and more" and then he gets the contract!

Please, without moving a product at a profit you can not maintain a business for very long.

Now there are folks who are in a NON/NOT for Profit business or maybe you work in Healthcare or the Government and the culture is just not oriented towards profit motive. That may very well be true, but that does not mean that you don't need to be profit motivated in what you do. At the very least your thinking and thought processes should be profit motivated.

So, if, for example, you or your teams work for a Church, how in the world, do you translate that into profit motive? Actually it's quite simple, a church just like a mom and pop Grocery store has a budget and a board of directors (maybe they call them regents or elders, its all the same), that must answer to the stock holders (the congregation). Therefore the board sets a budget and the working staff (that's you) has to do everything you can to keep costs down and profits up. Well since you technically don't have an income stream (or profit margin) than your job is to keep costs down and resources at their highest and best use. Depending on what you do (The choir director has a different view than the IT guy), you may be able to find new and exciting way to use the resources you have, maybe the choir director should advertise the choir is available for concerts, soundtracks or backgrounds for contributions. Where as the IT Guy's are going to do everything that they know how to do to keep costs down through the use of open source and again, potentially outsourcing themselves for contributions to the church.

Or you can sit back and read the Wall Street Journal or watch HNN and just thank your creator that you don't have to worry about THAT kind of "stuff." Of course you will want to give the guys a hand when they come to re - posses everything in the administration suite because the bills haven't been paid.

If you take the opportunity to become profit oriented in everything you and your team does for your company, the company will soon be calling you on a regular basis asking what else it is that they can get you to do for them. The bottom line is the priority in every business.

20) Develop POSITIVE personal power.

For years we have all been told that the key to personal success is through having and maintaining a positive mental attitude. So what's this about personal power? Sounds like a Tony Robbins program doesn't it?

They are somewhat related, actually one is an extension of the other, a large extension. Think of Personal Power as the end result of taking a positive attitude to its natural conclusion.

A Positive attitude is all about you developing a series of tools that you can pull out at anytime to change the frame of mind that you are in during that time. The challenge with a positive attitude is that other than make you smile, and allowing you to feel better even in the face of catastrophe it won't actually have anything other than "side effects" on those around you. It may amuse them, and it will definitely give them something else to talk about for a minute, but it may not actually **do** anything for your business.

What? Heresy! I know I grew up that way as well. But really just like "Faith without works are dead" a Positive mental attitude without an application of it, will yield very little. Other than people wondering if your "for real."

Once you have yourself in a positive frame of mind you need to now do something with it! For example let's say that you are an insurance salesman, on Monday you were ready to tear up the world and outsell the entire eastern seaboard. By Friday, you can barely lift your chin high enough to see over the steering wheel. But you know the magic of PMA, so you pop in a Zig tape on your way to the office and by the time you get there, you feel much better and have a much greater self expectation of yourself, your job and your abilities. But none of that matters if you don't actually do something with it!

So Mr. Insurance agent, what do you do to take your Attitude and convert it to Power?

Well you feel better so you probably have a smile in your voice if not actually on your face, now is the time to call some folks. They will be able to hear that smile and it will put them at ease. You know your business, you understand that it may take 100 calls to book 5 appointments, and since you have nothing setup for today you need at least 5 appointments. Plus, since you already have that smile on your face, which is showing in your voice, why not dig out those 5 or 10 folks who have always been nasty to you, and call them first. What? Why would you want to waste a perfectly good smile that way? Well very simply, you know that your positive attitude is contagious; you also know that nothing those folks can do or say will really have any effect on your day. So why not attack them first!

Personal power is what you need to keep you dialing through and smiling through all 100 phone calls. You can not stop at 90 you can not stop just when you have your first 5 appointments. You must power through and call all 100 people. There was a study done some time ago, and what they found is that many people in commission based jobs place a limit on themselves that has nothing to do with reality. John had a great year and earned $80,000 the most he had ever earned in his life. After that first big year he was NEVER able to top that income level. Regardless of whether he had the greatest or the worst territory in the company, he ended the year earning $80,000. Whether he had access to the newest products and techniques available, John saw himself as an $80,000 a year man, and even that only on a great year! He would do just enough to earn his $80,000 and then something always seemed to "happen." He got sick, or his car broke down, something always ended up interfering with his moving past it. He had created an artificial barrier between who he was, and what he was capable of doing. Don't fall prey to the same attitude. Even after your goals have been reached keep working through to the finish.

Wait, you mean even after I have all 5 of today's appointments I still have to keep dialing?

Absolutely, because why should your Monday (typically the toughest day of the week to have no Appointments) be as bad as your Friday started. So as soon as you get your 5 appointments, keep right on moving until you have made 100 calls. Trust me, on Monday you will thank me! Now, on Monday you won't have to spend all day before lunch trying to make yourself feel better, because unlike your friends, you already have appointments setup!

So yes, keep powering through. So, its 11am, you have just finished your list of calls, you have 5 appointments setup for after lunch. Now what? Now you need to stop and go straight to lunch, by yourself, and keep that Power moving and growing. Now you're done with lunch as most folks are just now starting theirs and off you go to the first of five appointments. Not cold calls, but customers that you have pre screened on the phone and who know why you're coming. What do you think your chances are of making a sale to a customer who knows when you're coming; why you're coming and whom you just spoke to a few hours ago. These customers all but invited them to their office! More importantly when you get there, not only will you be smiling but you will be standing straighter, have more power and enthusiasm in your voice and a complete knowledge of your product line in your head. Since you weren't planning on making any money anyway, your conversation will be much more natural than if you were "desperate" to make a sale. Now you know you're going to be making sales, the odds are on your side. Now how much of an advantage do you have over everyone else!

You have taken your positive attitude and placed it behind some positive action and now you are not only in a better place for today than you were when the day started, but you have a leg up on the next day's work as well! You now have Personal Power!

21) Become ACTION oriented.

Are you getting a little "disoriented" with all these different directions you now need to be moving towards? I know I am, and I developed them! But I also know that by changing who we are and what we do, we will soon find many of these items a natural outgrowth of who you are. This will show itself in your production, but even more importantly it will soon be evident in your team and in their actions and reactions. Again this almost seems too obvious to state, but unfortunately there are so many folks who just don't get this one, that it needs to be stated again.

Do not let a business idea enter your mind that you don't act upon. Even if your action is to just write it down! I can not begin to count the number of great ideas that I have had, only to find some hours, or days later, that they are gone. I understand that you can get so wrapped up in your day to day issues that you just forget about them. Even if you should remember a portion of what they were, they will have lost their luster and some of the key benefits, just by you having delayed making the note. Carry a notebook or a PDA and anytime an idea pops in your head, business related, jot it down. You will find that eventually you will need to find a way to organize them, and then you will need on a weekly basis, if not more often, to "dump" them from their original source out to something more permanent.

This is a great way to deal with wasting time as well. Don't handle your mail more than once, if a bill comes, pay it (you can wait to mail it until you have the money), if its an ad you're not interested in throw it away, if its something that you are interested in, that's where your organization comes in. Create 2 folders, one for mail that you must attend to this week, one that you can hold off on for a week, a month or more! Take action immediately.

Now I am going to give you two ideas that have the ability, within the next 10 days, to change your business life. Now I know that is a pretty bold statement and I do not make it lightly. However I also know it's a fact and if I told you how much money I lost before I implemented it, you either wouldn't believe me, or, like me, you would cry.

1) **Respond *immediately*:** You have people who contact you. A great majority of them can be considered customers. In this instance I am using customer in a definition that is outside what most people see when they hear the word. As a leader your customers come from many directions.

> a. If you work in a company as a member of the housekeeping staff. Your customers are every person in every area that you meet, talk to and who's areas you clean every day.
>
> b. If you are a Manager of an IS team in a major medical institution your customers are also everyone on your team.
>
> c. If you are a team member in an insurance company that sells mostly discounted Auto Insurance, you customers are every single person you see on any given day, who drives a car.
>
> d. If you are an Orthopedic Surgeon, your customers include every nurse, technician, and administrator in any and every hospital that you ever have or hope to have rights to practice with.

These cover a slightly more broad definition of the word customer than probably went through your mind the first time you heard me say the word didn't it? But that's the point we have customers in almost every corner of every space we are in on a daily basis. But because we do not treat them like they are bringing us a check for $10,000 we may never understand how much their business was worth over a lifetime! But these folks will be contacting you; most of them will do so over the phone. Caller ID is a great time savings tool. No longer do we have to be bothered every time we sit down to eat a meal. Unfortunately most folks abuse this tool. Most folks use it to answer the phone only when they "feel" like talking to that particular person.

I have a friend of mine who understands this use all to well. She looks at the caller ID every time the phone rings. Now I understand when she won't answer it if the call comes up as **private, blocked, 800#** or **unknown**. The part I don't get is when her "best friend calls" several times over a span of months and she doesn't answer the phone. Now we ALL have friends who don't know the foundries of a friendly phone call. But we should all know how to bring to a conclusion a call like that, "Wow look at that Suzy, its 6pm, I must get dinner ready for the boys."

But, even if you determine that you are just absolutely too busy to take that call, or if your driving – phones are way too distracting in the car, if you have voicemail and they leave a message make it your mission to call them back promptly! Once I started developing this as my habit I dedicated the hour between 8am and 9am every single morning, except Sunday, to returning phone calls. Most of those folks that I didn't really want to talk to weren't available during those hours anyway. The rest of them, I was able to make appointments with, and typically I would book the follow up appointment at the same time! Just as an example, the LAST time that I did not return a call promptly, before I changed my habits, cost me an $1800 booking fee. 'nuff said.

2) Respond not only **when** you said you would, but **after every contact** as well. If you email me and say that you need the XYS paperwork by tomorrow at noon, and I know it is going to take me every single minute up to noon to create that paperwork. You will hear from me at noon tomorrow, but that's not the only time. After I read your email I will immediately reply and reaffirm exactly what it was that you asked for, But if anything comes up in the meantime, I will email you about that as well. Additionally, I am going to email you a status update tomorrow morning, to let you know where we are and that we should have exactly what you need ready for you, when you need it. Finally, once the work is completed you will get the email containing the XYS paper work, and a thank you for the business email as well as an email the day following to make sure that it was what you wanted.

Once I understood this practice and implemented it, the only people who started to ask me why they were receiving so many emails were the folks who worked for me. See they knew that I had to have a reason for doing it, they just hadn't put the pieces together to figure out why. Some of them actually believed it was my way of "checking up on them." Believe me if I wanted to check yup on you, you wouldn't know it!

Finally something that should be almost self evident, if someone gives you a referral, call them as soon as you are out of ear shot of the person you received it from. Then once you have made your appointment, make sure that you contact the person that gave you the referral and thank them again for it. When you have met with the referral and concluded your business, contact the originator and once again thank them for the referral and, if appropriate, let them know how things went! People will only give you referrals if they think you are treating their friends as well as they would!

Take action, take immediate action and take appropriate action. You world will change for the better in 10 days or less!

AFTERWORD

Well here we are 200 pages later, if you are an employee looking to place your career on the fast track and make it automatic, then you should certainly have the tools that you need to accomplish that.

If however, you are in management, and you have read this far, I think that you should have everything you need to keep your career moving as fast as you want it to grow, in the direction that you want it to grow. Additionally I hope that you understand that just because you have several folks on your team that you want to promote, but who may be lacking one or two skills, you have found the tools here, to make that decision properly.

Finally if you are an Entrepreneur or a small business owner and are seeking to understand your friends, family or customers better, I believe you now have the tools to do that better. But more importantly, I believe that you now have the tools that you need to not just create new customers, but to develop the relationships with people who will return to you, and look forward to doing so. As you look around you will find that people are happy to come back to you, and you may even sense that 'sigh of relief in their voice when the phone rings and they realize that it's you on the other end.

Finally if you are reading this because you really want to help someone who is just starting out in their career, and your not quite sure how to help them, hopefully telling them about this book, or giving them a copy, will give them the resources they need to get started on their fast track to corporate success.

Resources

The resources used to create a book like this come from over 30 years in business in almost every possible role. In a single company, I have gone from entry level at $10/ hour to management (six figures) in 5 years. All while using the tools and techniques in these books.

However, I refuse to even try and take credit for myself; instead I'd like to introduce you to some of MY mentors.

I had a young lady; a few years ago tell me for over an hour, how much she wanted to "be just like me." Yet when I referred her to the areas where I gained my abilities, suddenly her career wasn't that important anymore. So please, take my word for it these are some folks you want to "meet" and some books you want to read.

Dale Carnegie: *How to Win Friends and Influence People:*

I knew someone once who *refused* to read this because they were "not interested in controlling other people". After several hours of trying to explain it's actually about getting along with folks, I gave up. Truly one of the greats, if you can find an original copy, get it, the information from the 1930's is just as relevant as today, and a lot more fun to read.

Andy Andrews: *The Noticer:*

I was lucky enough to meet Andy and Polly when he was just getting started in public speaking and before his writing had begun. This was while he was still Americas #1 College Comedian. This book is the beginning of a wonderful exploration of an entire series of discoveries that you may find yourself on, and one that he is well equipped to lead.

Og Mandino: *The Greatest Miracle in the World:*

For years my dad tried to get me to read The Greatest Salesman in the World, and I could just never finish it. However, I finished this book in less than a few days and it had a profound impact on my life. However I do tell folks that if you buy it and read it, it's a good story, if you buy it and out it on a shelf until you think that you can't go any farther than you are, you may discover the miracle

Forty Years at the Feet of the Worlds Greatest Mentor:

My dad passed away a few years ago, yet every day I am rediscovering the wisdom that he tried to team me every single day. The one thing I know I did was, on occasion I disappointed him. But he always gave me the chance to stand up, dust myself off and start all over again. The one tool that he gave me that has been worth more that anything else in the world was this: Getting knocked down by life or work or people is *not* the end of the world. Staying down **is.**

Other books in this Series

Remote Control Professional:

The Remote Control term came to me one day, on my way out the door when I realized that I had finally achieved the state of mind with a team that I could relax and know that everything would be "all right" while I was gone. Not a feeling most managers get from their teams. However, anything can be a fluke, so I started to make note of the things that I did that were different from what the other managers were doing. Then at my next management opportunity I started all over again with a new team and new folks and the same tools. They too reached the remote control stage.

Then I started to teach some of my fellow managers some of the techniques that I was using, amazingly enough they received the same results. Science is all about duplicateable results.

Remote Control Entrepreneur:

What happens when you finally reach that pinnacle of achievement, that golden carrot with a corner window and rubber tree plant and youre still not feeling fulfilled by what you do 5 days a week?

Read **Remote Control Entrepreneur** and find out not only WHAT I did, but how I did It, the resources I used, and the lessons learned all along the way.

A step by step playbook for developing the business called:

YOUR OWN

Out of Control Networking:

Early on I was introduced to Network Marketing, although back then it was plain old MLM. I learned many lessons along the way to finding my place in the world of business owndersip. Cheif among them is that anytime a mentor offers you 5 minutes, take advantage of all 5 minutes.

Next, when given the opportunity to speak, you do not have to take advantage of it. Additonally you dont have to reinvent the wheel to be successful. If 30 years of folks have come before you and been successful at doing something, what makes you think you have a better idea?

The national Franchisors Association has once again noted that the one career that the most successful Franchise owner comes from, is that of a farmer. Farmers know that they don't know, and they are willing to learn how to do what they want to acheive. After reading **Out of Control Networking** I think that you too will have the toolbox that you need, in order to be completely succesful in whatever it is that you decide to do,

.

Remote Control Management

www.ingramcontent.com/pod-product-compliance
Lightning Source LLC
Chambersburg PA
CBHW070646160426
43194CB00009B/1593